IMAGINATION IN KANT'S
Critique of Practical Reason

STUDIES IN
CONTINENTAL THOUGHT

JOHN SALLIS, GENERAL EDITOR

IMAGINATION IN KANT'S
Critique of Practical Reason

Bernard Freydberg

INDIANA UNIVERSITY PRESS

Bloomington and Indianapolis

This book is a publication of

Indiana University Press
601 North Morton Street
Bloomington, IN 47404-3797 USA

http://iupress.indiana.edu

Telephone orders   800-842-6796
Fax orders   812-855-7931
Orders by e-mail   iuporder@indiana.edu

The paper used in this publication meets the minimum requirements of Ameri-
can National Standard for Information Sciences—Permanence of Paper for
Printed Library Materials, ANSI Z39.48-1984.

Manufactured in the United States of America

Library of Congress Cataloging-in-Publication Data

Library of Congress Cataloging-in-Publication Data

Freydberg, Bernard, date
Imagination in Kant's Critique of practical reason / Bernard Freydberg.
p. cm. — (Studies in Continental thought)
Includes bibliographical references and index.
ISBN 0-253-34641-X (alk. paper) — ISBN 0-253-21787-3 (pbk. : alk. paper)
1. Kant, Immanuel, 1724-1804. Kritik der praktischen Vernunft. 2. Ethics.
3. Practical reason. 4. Imagination. I. Title. II. Series.
B2774.F74 2005
170—dc22

2005011534

1 2 3 4 5   10 09 08 07 06 05

For John Sallis
Without whom, nothing.

CONTENTS

Acknowledgments

Philosophy has the delightfully paradoxical quality that while the writing is done in solitude, every philosophical work is dialogical in many ways. This book, of course, is no exception. Imagination in Kant's *Critique of Practical Reason* owes its initial impetus to my two great Kant teachers, John Sallis and the late Lewis White Beck. The former planted seeds that continue to grow and showed me avenues of thought that I continue to follow out. The latter exposed me to both the power of Kantian thought and to thoroughgoing scholarly rigor. My colleague and friend Richard Findler at Slippery Rock University read this entire text and offered his characteristically insightful criticisms, making this a better book.

I also have the great good fortune of membership in a philosophy department that combines vigorous exchange of ideas with deep friendship. In addition to Richard Findler, ongoing conversations with William Oman and Bradley Wilson and emeritus professors Allan Larsen and Theodore Kneupper have been important in very many ways. Three library staff members, Kathleen Manning, Kevin McLatchy, and Rita McClelland, provided help far beyond the call of duty.

I gladly acknowledge the contribution of the many fine students, past and present, whom I have been privileged to teach. Special mention goes to Michael Rudar, now a graduate student with a most promising philosophical future, who read the copy of the final manuscript. I am also grateful for the support of the entire Slippery Rock University administration.

The Indiana University Press editorial staff has provided invaluable aid of its own. With a blend of insight and directness that somehow makes it a pleasure to accept criticism, Dee Mortensen, sponsoring editor of Indiana University Press, has substantially improved this book's final form. Her two readers, whose names I do not know, offered both encouraging praise and helpful, often incisive remarks that enabled me to make changes for the better. Elisabeth M. Marsh, assistant sponsoring editor, provided generous and expert help in the preparation of the final manuscript.

Finally, I acknowledge my two greatest gifts of good fortune. I thank my daughter, Malika Hadley Freydberg, for her courage and her openness. For her insights on imagination and for the daily inspiration I receive from her presence in my life, I thank my wife, Akiko Kotani.

Note on the Text and on Page References

All page references to the *Critique of Practical Reason* (*Kritik der prak-tischen Vernunft*) are drawn from *Kants Werke. Akademie Textausgabe*, Band V. Berlin, 1968. These will read, both in the main text and in the notes, "V, page number." Page references to the *Critique of Pure Reason* (*Kritik der reinen Vernunft*) are made to both editions (e.g., A78, B101), except when the passage cited appears in one edition but not the other. The Transcendental Deductions in each shall be re-ferred to as "A Deduction" and "B Deduction" respectively.

The translation I most often cite, though with changes where these seem appropriate and indicating the German, is Immanuel Kant, *Cri-tique of Practical Reason*, trans. Lewis White Beck, Indianapolis and New York, 1956. References to the *Akademie* edition are included in the text.

IMAGINATION IN KANT'S
Critique of Practical Reason

From the *Critique of Pure Reason* to the *Critique of Practical Reason*

Between Kant's two "larger" critiques, the *Critique of Pure Reason* (884 of Kant's pages for the 2nd edition) and the *Critique of Judgment* (482 pages), sits the quantitatively meager (163 page) *Critique of Practical Reason*. Despite the proportionally greater attention paid by scholars to the quantitatively larger critiques, it could not be clearer that the middle, moral critique held the highest significance for Kant. This is so not only because he expressly proclaimed "The Primacy of the Practical," but because both its predecessor and its successor in the critical philosophy gave unmistakable indications as well.

On the final page of the Final Purpose of the Natural Dialectic of Human Reason in the *Critique of Pure Reason*, Kant calls the resolution of all of our transcendent knowledge into its elements valuable, and "to the philosopher . . . indeed a *matter of duty*" (A703, B731, emphasis mine). As action from duty is the only acceptable moral intention, it therefore follows that the entire undertaking of the first critique took place under the sway of a moral command. On the final page of the Critique of the Aesthetical Judgment in the *Critique of Judgment*, Kant writes that "it appears plain that the true propaedeutic for the foundation of taste is the development of moral ideas and the culture of the moral feeling, because it is only when sensibility is brought into agreement with this that genuine taste can assume an invariable form" (V, 356).

In this book I shall attempt not only to take Kant's own words on the centrality of the *Critique of Practical Reason* more seriously than is usually the case, but I shall also attempt to show, by means of this initial chapter and later by means of the concluding chapter, (1) how the *Critique of Pure Reason* should and must be read as leading up to and opening onto the *Critique of Practical Reason,* and (2) how the *Critique of Practical Reason* leads up to and opens onto the *Critique of Judgment.* Would that this task be as straightforward as it sounds! Instead, a painstaking and, at least apparently, radical interpretation of the *Critique of Practical Reason* itself is required in order to display the flow of the three critiques as indicated above.

Why is such an interpretation required? As my title has already disclosed, *imagination* shall serve as the abiding fulcrum of the critical philosophy in general and of the three critiques in particular. There is little difficulty in locating defining passages in the *Critique of Pure Reason* and in the *Critique of Judgment* that would place imagination at their hearts. However, in the *Critique of Practical Reason,* Kant specifically and directly *excludes* imagination from having any role in practical philosophy.

This exclusion is no doubt at least partially responsible for the reputation of coldness, dryness, mechanism, excessive rationality, etc., that has attached to Kant's moral philosophy. It would seem, also, to put special and perhaps insurmountable obstacles before an interpreter like myself who wishes to claim both (1) that imagination is the single, unique element that unites the three critiques and that (2) the *Critique of Practical Reason* provides the linchpin of that unity. Yet that is exactly what I propose.

Readers with an interest in how this interpretation relates to the work of other scholars and how their scholarship bears upon this interpretation can find discussions and dialogues, some of which are extensive, in the endnotes. The book, however, can be read straight through.

* * *

The following sentence occurs in the final paragraph of the Introduction of the *Critique of Pure Reason:*

Prologue

> Only so much seems to be needed (*nötig*) by way of introduction or anticipation (*Vorerrinerung*) [to both divisions of the *Critique of Pure Reason*], that there are two stems of human knowing (*Erkenntnis*) that perhaps spring from a common, but to us unknown root, namely *sensibility* and *understanding;* through the former objects are *given* to us, but through the latter they are *thought.* (A15, B29)

This sentence has attracted much attention as a result of Heidegger's famously dramatic and surprising reading according to which *imagination* is this root. The responses to it have been many and various, although this reading, by virtue at least of its power and also, to many, of its insight, has become less radical over the years. Those who ignore it, hoping that it will disappear, do so in vain.[1]

However, I propose to pay attention not merely to the matter of the stems of human knowing and to the root that they perhaps share, but to the sentence as a whole. First of all, Kant claims in it that this division of the stems applies *both* to the Doctrine of Elements *and* to the Doctrine of Method. The former is occupied primarily with matters concerning the nature and limits of human theoretical knowing within the fundamental questions of metaphysics,[2] although its reach exceeds even that enormous task. But the latter, the Doctrine of Method, is concerned just as much or more with matters concerning *practical* philosophy. The distinction between sensibility and understanding, and their possible issue from a common but to us unknown root, then, concerns *practical* reason at the very outset.

In this book, I will show how imagination runs through the *Critique of Practical Reason* as its mostly concealed and silent but nevertheless guiding thread. In order to do so, it is necessary for me to exhibit, in a general way, how imagination in its practical function can be traced out in the *Critique of Pure Reason*. This will require an overview of the latter in terms of imagination. The overview shall be presented schematically, in terms of what will look very much like a valid (also sound) logical argument. However, the matters lie far deeper than mere logic, at least formal (in Kant's word "general") logic, can reach.

Even though specific textual issues cannot be given much space in such a brief survey, I claim that this survey uncovers what might be called the "central nervous system" of the critical philosophy. Its irreducible "center of the center" is called *synthesis*. Following the above analogy, synthesis activates the neurons so that they can do their work with any coherence at all.

> Synthesis in general (*überhaupt*) as we shall hereafter see, is the result of the power of imagination, a blind but indispensable function of the soul, without which we would have no knowledge whatsoever, but of which we are scarcely ever conscious. (A78, B103)

It is the function of understanding "to bring this synthesis *to concepts*" by means of which we get "knowledge *properly so called*" (A78, B103, emphasis mine). By means of sensibility we receive intuitions, i.e., representations given in space and time. As "all thought must . . . directly or indirectly, relate ultimately to intuitions, and therefore with us, to sensibility" (A19, B33), all knowledge properly so called consists of the putting-together, the syn-thesis,[3] of concepts and intuitions.

In the *Critique of Practical Reason*, "knowledge properly so called" is not present. "Practical knowledge" does not arise through any relation of concepts and intuitions. Rather, as will be discussed in the main part of this book, only by means of the extension of the nonsensible idea of freedom can human knowledge reach into the practical realm of the supersensible. Further, this extension occurs only by means of the *act* whereby that idea of freedom is asserted as real. While the moral law and moral judgments are determinative, i.e., they really do determine objective principles of action, these judgments contain no reference to sensibility—and hence are not "knowledge properly so called."

"Knowledge properly so called" is also absent in the *Critique of Judgment*. The judgment of taste is a reflective rather than a determinant judgment. It refers the feeling of the subject back to its own faculties of representation, and neither to the natural nor to the moral realm. In other words, it has a determining ground that is "*no other than subjective*" (V, 4, 203,[4] emphasis in original). The teleological judgment also "belongs to the reflective and not to the determinant judgment" (V, 269, 360).[5] The claim that nature is purposively designed is expressly *not* made. Rather, the concept of the purposive-ness of nature is a subjective principle in accord with which the in-vestigations of nature can be guided by a concern for rule-governed unity.

Thus, the possibility of "knowledge properly so called" is estab-lished only in the first of the three critiques. However, *synthesis* beats at the heart of all three. And as synthesis is the "mere result of the power of imagination" (*Einbildungskraft*), imagination is the heart-beat of all three critiques. What is imagination? Kant gives sev-eral different formulations during the course of the *Critique of Pure Reason*.[6] Whatever their differences, all share imagination's *synthetic* function. This function will be carried forward into the subsequent two critiques, into the *Critique of Judgment,* where its importance is obvious, and even more tellingly into the *Critique of Practical Reason,* where it might seem to have no importance at all.

As has been observed particularly by Sallis, the *Critique of Pure Reason* is a heterogeneous text.[7] First of all, the subject matter driv-ing the text consists of the aforementioned two heterogeneous stems of knowledge: sensibility, which consists of our capacity to receive representations in space and time (intuitions), and understanding, which consists of our capacity to provide unity to our intuitions (concepts). To the former, the name "receptivity" belongs; the latter is called "spontaneity."

However, the heterogeneity of the Kantian text goes far deeper than even this already provocative division. "Pure intuition," the key notion that arises from the Transcendental Aesthetic (the very first part of the Transcendental Doctrine of Elements), contains both strains of a supposedly unbridgeable chasm within itself. Still fur-ther, the double abstraction (first from the understanding and its con-cepts, then from empirical sensibility) that allows the Aesthetic to unfold seems similarly problematic. In the following paragraphs, I shall lay out the Kantian doctrine of pure intuition and interpret the double abstraction in such a way that the Kantian text, despite its heterogeneous nature, not only retains but also enhances its integrity.

As indicated in the above citation from A19, B33, for us humans, all thought must ultimately relate to sensibility (intuition). Since the latter requires that the object be given to us, i.e., that "the mind is affected in a certain way" (A19, B33), human intuition is, almost by definition here, *empirical* intuition. But Kant writes the following only a few paragraphs later: "I term all representations *pure* (in the transcendental sense) in which there is nothing that belongs to sensation" (A20, B34, emphasis in original). Assuming that all our intuition is empirical, i.e., bound to sensation, and the notion "pure" can be applied only to those representations that contain nothing of sensation, whatever can "pure intuition" mean?

One recourse (the recourse adopted by one of my great Kant teachers, Lewis White Beck) is to note the contradiction, then charitably and reasonably suggest that the phrase "pure intuition" be read as "pure *form of intuition*." This option accomplishes three ends in one bold stroke: it removes a most embarrassing contradiction; it replaces the contradiction with what Kant almost surely meant; it renders coherent the entire doctrine of sensibility. In my view, however, one objection overrides all the obvious virtues of Beck's "remedy." Kant never veered from "pure intuition" as the expression for the *a priori* representations of space and time, and had he wished to, "pure form of intuition" stood before him as an obvious alternative.

The term "pure intuition" contains within it an obvious *tension,* but as will be shown, far from being a contradiction, this tension is one of the animating spurs that drive the critical philosophy beyond the tasks Kant sets for it. Beyond bringing the prior rationalisms of Descartes, Leibniz, and Spinoza together with the empiricisms of Locke, Berkeley, and Hume, beyond saving metaphysics from the endless strife to which it has been subject, beyond the "transcendental logical" discovery of synthetic *a priori* judgments and their abiding role in both securing and limiting human knowledge, the notion of pure intuition drives the critical philosophy beyond even *itself.*

The reading of a person's *intentions,* even when the person herself or himself does this reading, is fraught with difficulty by its very nature. It is a venture into the dark, closed off from certainty and perhaps even from probability given the unconscious motives to which all human beings are subject. Accordingly, a *great thinker's* intentions are, *a fortiori*, difficult to accomplish—likely much more so than those of the rest of us.

However, in the case of Kant and pure intuition, the intent is quite clear to me, even if the result seems logically puzzling. Kant's sole aim was to let the evidence lead wherever it would and, as Heidegger said, never to feign light where there is darkness. Since intuition requires givenness, a *pure* intuition must be *an intuition that we give ourselves*. It is clear that we do not and cannot give ourselves sensible objects themselves. Nor can we give ourselves intelligible objects, objects of reason apart from sensation. These are altogether closed off from our knowing. However, we can and do give ourselves the form(s) by virtue of which sensible objects, objects as appearances, are possible for us.

Space and time are these forms. As Kant argues, they are not things in themselves, as Newton maintained. Nor are they mere relations of objects that are merely properties of our subjective nature, without which they would not be ascribable to anything, as Leibniz supposed. Rather, they are the real sensible forms of our knowledge. With regard to things in themselves, the two pure intuitions are nothing at all. With regard to objects as appearances, with regard, i.e., to the human realm, they are objectively valid.

What is the ontological status of space and time? They are clearly not concepts in the strict sense. As Kant points out, concepts include many representations *under* themselves while intuitions include many representations *within* themselves. Thus the concept "red" includes apples, fire engines, blood, etc., and the [pure] concept "cause and effect" includes any event in which one appearance follows another according to a rule. "Space," by contrast, includes all spaces *within* it. Nor are these pure intuitions empirical "objects," given their purity. Perhaps they might be best characterized preliminarily as "*pure images,*" hovering[8] between the empirical intuitions they make possible and the concepts that confer knowledge properly so called.

Products neither of the sensibility nor the understanding, yet bringing together the characteristics of both that are necessary conditions for experience and knowledge, pure intuitions are products of imagination. They can be counted both as falling within the Kantian problematic and as existing beyond its frame, making that frame possible at all.

Since all outer intuitions are also contained in us as inner intuitions, all of our intuitions are subject to time. Time comes, then, to be regarded as the form of all intuition. As the *Critique of Pure Reason* progresses, time and pure intuition become employed almost synonymously. This becomes especially important when imagination surfaces most prominently again, in the later Schematism of the Pure Concepts of the Understanding.

Kant presents the Pure Concepts of the Understanding (the Categories) as if they were derived from the admittedly awkward Table of Judgments,[9] which he regarded as the functions of judgment for general (i.e., formal) logic. If one were to characterize the movement from general logic to its transcendental "derivative," one might use the formula "general logic plus pure intuition equals transcendental logic." However, the order in which matters in the text are *presented* does not mirror the order of the subject matter *itself*.

Recall the double abstraction in the Transcendental Aesthetic alluded to above. In order to reach pure intuition, Kant proposed first to abstract from everything belonging to the understanding, and then to abstract from everything belonging to empirical intuition. The remainder would then be pure intuition. However, the necessary conditions for this double abstraction include (1) our thoroughgoing, unreflective immersion in concept building and (2) its counterpart in empirical intuition. In order to make sense of the arguments at all, we can totally let go neither of concepts nor of empirical intuitions. Indeed, without them we would have no experience at all, nothing.

When we look into the depths of our experience, we see further that without this strange creature called "pure intuition," the intuition that secures our only immediate relation to the world, we would have no access at all to knowledge properly so called. Further, without this pure image, without imagination, all access to experience would be closed off to us. As we form the most elementary and obvious judgments in our experience in the world, e.g., "rainwater is wet," imagination is already thoroughly and deeply at work. This is the case even in tautologies, such as "A is A."

Analogously, the equation "formal logic plus pure intuition equals transcendental logic" is misleading, although the order in the text seems to suggest its appropriateness. Rather, pure intuition is *always already at work*. If I were to rewrite the equation in a manner more faithful to the subject matter itself, it would read "transcendental logic *minus* pure intuition equals general logic." Imagination, pure intuition, transcendental logic, constitute the *first* encounter with objects of experience both ontologically and epistemologically, and provide the necessary condition for there to be such an encounter at all.

I return to the conceptual content of transcendental logic. Just as with pure intuitions, the pure concepts of the understanding taken together (the Table of Categories) constitute the necessary presupposition of the logical concepts of judgment, and not the reverse. This is so because all our thought has always already occurred under the sway of these pure concepts. That transcendental logic is driven by imagination, as established above, is assumed as given in all that follows.

I choose as an example the most contentious of the pure concepts, causality. If we were incapable of first placing one object before another in a necessary time-sequence (an event), we would be entirely at a loss to conceive the logical relation expressed in a hypothetical (if . . . then) judgment.[10]

This simple but hardly easy or insignificant insight belongs at once to Kant's general criticism of dogmatic metaphysics[11] and to his answer to Hume's challenge. In dogmatic metaphysics, the logical law of non-contradiction plays a positive role and is used to provide affirmative answers from reason alone to all the fundamental questions of metaphysics: Does God exist? Is the human soul immortal? Is the human will free? A rational ontology, containing the principles of all being, also belongs to dogmatic metaphysics.[12] However, as is well-known, Hume's skepticism convinced Kant that none of these affirmative conclusions were justified, that the claims of dogmatic metaphysics could not be defended against the equally logical claims of their negations.

Kant's general answer to Hume's skepticism regarding causality, an answer that fully grasps its cogency and its power and that such skepticism extends to all metaphysical questions, is as follows: Hume claimed that what one called "cause and effect" was at bottom nothing more than constant conjunction in time, accompanied by the belief that this constant conjunction would continue to obtain in the future. This was an *epistemological* claim. Hume never doubted that constant conjunctions, such as the onset of fire and the sensation of heat, would continue. He maintained only that no argument could be made that would render such confidence intelligible.

The key to Kant's argument is that in order for Hume to claim that only "constant conjunctions plus belief" could withstand philosophical scrutiny, Hume *had to presuppose* a necessary, law-bound time order in order to discern constant conjunctions at all. Thus, Hume tacitly presupposed the transcendental-logical pure concept of causality in order to be able to offer his skeptical arguments.

It is worthy of note that in his psychological description of causality, Hume himself places imagination at its heart. In accounting for the impression that must lie at the basis of every idea and that misleads us to the idea of cause and effect, Hume writes the following: "This connexion, therefore, which we *feel* in the mind, this customary transition of the *imagination* from one object to its usual attendant, is the sentiment or impression from which we form the idea of power or necessary connexion. Nothing farther is the case"[13] (emphasis on "feel" in original; emphasis on "imagination" mine).

Note that this imagination-governed impression is a far cry from Hume's earlier description of impressions as immediate and more lively contacts with sensation, and from his dismissal of the products of imagination as less lively than those that come from impressions. (Here there is no question—if indeed there can be any—that Hume was a philosophical giant and that his texts also point beyond themselves by virtue of their own rigor.) One would do well to see Kant's pure imagination as grounding the psychological imagination of Hume; just as the concept of a necessary time-order (cause and effect) is presupposed for there to be constant conjunction, so the synthesis of imagination whereby pure concepts and pure intuitions are joined is presupposed for the (empirical) imagination to move from one conjunct to the other.

Even granting the importance of the Transcendental Deduction of the Categories, to which Kant devoted many arduous years of work and within which—as I will soon show—imagination plays the central role once again, imagination is still not *fully* heard as the heartbeat of the *Critique of Pure Reason*.[14] The two versions of the Transcendental Deduction seem to differ widely. The A Deduction clearly places imagination at its heart, while the B Deduction neither treats it as extensively nor, it seems, as centrally. This difference has provided and continues to provide a feast for Kant scholars of all stripes, including myself. For the purposes of this Prologue, which aims merely at exhibiting how the first critique unfolds into the second in terms of imagination, the following brief account should suffice. I select the B Deduction, as I always do, for it provides the more difficult philosophical assignment.

While Kant seems to ascribe a power of synthesis to the understanding early in the B Deduction, this ascription occurs within an initial two-faculty approach: understanding as spontaneous (with apperception, the "I think," as its highest principle) and sensibility as receptive. The advantage of such an approach merely consists in ease of understanding. Also, just as earlier, the serial order of presentation in the text and the order in the actual subject matter can be and often are very different.

The Deduction proper, in my view, does not begin until §24. The prior sections, §15–§23, serve merely to set up the crucial move, which consists of the introduction of pure imagination. To speak more properly, the textual introduction of pure imagination serves to disclose its abiding presence and centrality all along, even and perhaps especially when it received no mention.

The title of §24 is "The Application of the Categories to Objects of the Senses in General." This title cannot be regarded merely as one beside the others. Rather, this title announces the answer to the animating question of the deduction itself, namely how the categories can apply to objects of the senses in the face of their entirely different origin. The argument is complex, but there is a one-word response: *imagination*.

> The understanding . . . in respect of the manifold which may be given to it in accordance with the form of sensible intuition, is able to determine sensibility inwardly. Thus the understanding, under the title of a *transcendental synthesis of imagination,* performs the act upon the *passive* subject, whose faculty it is. (B153–54, emphases in original)

In this way, Kant answers the question of how the categories relate to objects of the senses in general. But why, one might ask, does Kant append the words "in general" to the title of §24? He does so because the necessary specification concerning how each category relates to pure intuition, i.e., time, is lacking. The latter task belongs to the Schematism of the Pure Concepts of the Understanding. Only by means of the schemata, Kant claims, do the categories "possess *significance*" (*Bedeutung*) (A146, B185, emphasis in original).[15]

The categories are, perhaps curiously, regarded as insignificant without their schemata because they can determine no particular experience, although they can set out its general determining conditions. Even these general conditions, as I have indicated above, require pure imagination. But the schemata of the pure concepts have as their precise purpose the connection of the specific categories to pure intuition.

"*The schema is in itself always a product of imagination*" (A140, B179, emphasis mine). What Kant refers to as the schematism of the pure understanding must therefore be understood as parallel to his placing the transcendental synthesis of imagination above understanding: imagination's act upon the pure concepts of the understanding provides their schematism. The schemata are one and all transcendental time-determinations, bridging the categories and pure intuition not only in general ways as imagination did in the Deduction, but in application to specific modes of time.

The Schematism section will be treated extensively in the main part of this book. It is enough to note for now (and to bear in mind) this unusual characteristic of the schemata of the pure concepts of understanding (these schemata are listed in the note):[16]

> The schema of a *pure* concept of the understanding can never be brought to any image whatsoever. It is simply the pure synthesis, determined by a rule of that unity, in accordance with concepts, to which the category gives expression. (A142, B181, emphasis in original)

Once again employing "cause and effect" as example, there can be no *image* of cause, the way there can be an image of a triangle or of a dog. "Triangle" is an original whose image can be constructed in accord with its concept, and "dog," while a more vague original, allows for the construction of some kind of image (perhaps an inaccurate one) in accord with its schema "a four-footed animal." "Cause and effect" is a different kind of original. It has a schema, namely "the real upon which, whenever posited, something else always follows" (A144, B183). But this schema has as *its* role the reading of any objects of the senses and their possible images. We never sense "cause" at all. Rather, by virtue of the transcendental schemata, products of pure imagination, we are able to find meaning and significance in the world of sense, and we are able to discern images, at all. For example, only by means of the category of causality can we read the onset of fire as the cause of the feeling of heat, rather than, e.g., that same onset with the meal some fires have a role in preparing, or with some random, unrelated occurrence that follows its onset.

As my snapshot of the Schematism ends and I move into discussion of the Principles of the Pure Understanding, it is worth reminding once again that the serial order of the text and the order of the subject matter are far from one and the same. Every example employed for any reason, every sentence in this book, presupposes the presence of the transcendental schemata, and therefore the working of pure imagination. Once again, imagination's synthetic function drives the entire critical philosophy, even and perhaps especially when it does not receive mention. Especially worthy of note here, however, is the additional service provided by imagination. While it surely *drives* human knowledge, it simultaneously *limits* this knowledge to those objects made possible by pure intuition, namely *appearances*. Of things in themselves, neither imagination nor the categories nor intuition can beget any knowledge at all.

The Principles (*Grundsätze*) of the Pure Understanding are the synthetic *a priori* principles that ultimately make knowledge possible. By their means, we can have secure theoretical (scientific) knowledge, but only of appearances. Their self-limiting nature, assured by the major role of imagination, guarantees that the key claims of traditional metaphysics (God exists, the soul is immortal, the human will is free) cannot be knowledge claims.

For purposes of this book, however, the section on the Principles should be read in terms of imagination's bringing together of all the prior derived elements in terms of their application to experience. In order of their textual presentation, these elements are pure intuition (time), pure concepts of the understanding (the categories), and the pure schemata. As I have attempted to prove, only by virtue of pure imagination do the categories connect with time to provide the conditions for experience in general, and only by virtue of pure imagination do the categories, by means of their schemata, connect determinately with pure intuition.

In the section on the Principles, the concern is the connection of these pure elements to actual appearances, i.e., the demonstration that these pure connections are connections that make actual human experience possible. The two Mathematical Principles connect appearances to *magnitude*, first extensive then intensive (they are the first two listed in the note).[17] Both principles are synthetic, both connect the pure concepts of Quantity and Quality to "all appearances," and both can do so only by the connection of the category to pure intuition by means of the schemata.

The Dynamical Principles are the last two groups listed in the note. Each group has three members. The first, the Analogies of Experience, concern *relations* of the categories to appearances. The second, the Postulates, concern empirical judgment in relation to the human subject. *Causality* is the category contained in the Second Analogy of Experience. Only by means of the category's schema cited above, "the real upon which, whenever posited, something else always follows," enables us to distinguish rule-governed from accidental connections at all. As the schema is in itself always a product of imagination, the inevitable but certainly not uninteresting conclusion follows necessarily that only imagination enables us to exercise correct discernment in such crucial matters.

Regarding the Postulates of Empirical Thought, I shall only make the following two observations. Possibility, Actuality, and Necessity one and all refer to their relation to the subject in terms of *perception*. As Kant has shown in his argument for the principle of the Axioms of Intuition (the first Mathematical Principle),

> Even the perception of an object, as appearance, is only possible through the same synthetic unity of the manifold of intuition as that whereby the unity of the combination of the manifold . . . is thought in the concept of a *magnitude*. (A162, B203)

Synthesis means *imagination*. Imagination, as has been shown, is also responsible for the *self-limiting* character of the critical philosophy. The primary importance of the Postulates, an importance derived from their tie to perception and thus to imagination, is to guarantee this self-limitation through a Principle.

But can there be a guarantee? It seems not. As Kant wrote in the famous opening words of the Preface to the first edition of the *Critique of Pure Reason*, "Human reason has this peculiar fate that in one species of its knowledge it is burdened by questions which, as prescribed by the very nature of reason itself, it is not able to ignore, but which, as transcending all its powers, it is also not able to answer" (Avii). The questions to which we are driven by our nature but whose answers are withheld from us in principle are, once again, the questions of special metaphysics concerning God, the soul, and the freedom of the human will. In terms of language I have not yet employed in this Prologue but which is well-known and in some sense restates its conclusion, we have knowledge only of *phenomena*, i.e., of things as they appear.

The final section from the *Critique of Pure Reason* that I will consider is the section on Phenomena and Noumena, and in particular the concealed role of imagination in it. The Dialectic will be treated fully in the earlier sections of the main part of this book. To make the matter as straightforward as possible, "phenomenon" means "object as appearance," and "noumenon" means "object of reason." ("*Phainesthai*" means "to appear"; "*Nous*" is here translated as "reason.") (For now, I leave aside the matter of the relation between noumena and things in themselves, which will be treated in a note in the main part of this book.)

The governing synthesis and syntheses of imagination have demonstrated that our knowledge is restricted to phenomena. We have no knowledge of noumena. I have also suggested the necessary role of imagination in constructing the edifice whereby we at once attain the knowledge that lies within our grasp and hold back from claiming any knowledge that lies beyond it.

The condition for the possibility of phenomena arises from the imagination-driven bond of the categories to intuition. Of course not a single concrete empirical phenomenon is determined by the pure apparatus, but can only be given through empirical intuition. How, then, does a noumenon arise? According to Kant, noumena arise when the categories are supposedly freed *from* the bond to intuition. Negative noumenon = "*not an object of our sensible intuition.*" Positive noumenon = "*object of a non-sensible intuition*" (both B307, both emphases in original). The negative noumenon is in complete accord with the limits established by the critical philosophy. The positive noumenon, since we humans do not have a non-sensible (i.e., intellectual) intuition, is not, and it provides a danger to the integrity of the former, at least with respect to the *theoretical* side of the critical philosophy.

The danger resides in the *thinkability* of the noumena. After all, the three noumena that result from the freeing of the categories from the bond to intuition one and all involve no contradiction, and this is thinkability's only criterion. More specifically, when the categories of substance, cause, and community are released from their bond to intuition and become the *ideas* of the soul, the world (problematically including free will), and God, there is no difficulty in *thinking* them together with their most suggestive predicates (immortality, freedom, and existence respectively). The danger is that the possibility of the thought of these propositions will be mistakenly confused with the possibility of knowing them, or worse, with actual knowledge of what they state.

In the freeing of the bond to sensation in the generation of the noumena, can we say that imagination has somehow been subtracted from, or is absent from, the conception of the noumena and their important metaphysical propositions? In one sense, we can: the schematism is no longer operative, nor is the transcendental synthesis of imagination through whose title the pure understanding joins with pure intuition.

However, the "freed" categories-become-ideas receive their meaning only by virtue of their connection to predicates in synthetic *a priori* judgments of another kind. "The soul is immortal," "the human will is free," and "God exists" are one and all synthetic, and so one and all require imagination. Still further, although we have to *think* them as part of our "metaphysical fate," we have the means both to avoid the risk they present and to put them to positive use. That risk, in Socratic terms, is the risk of claiming to know and perhaps pretending to know that which we do not and cannot know. That positive use concerns their moral role, as will be seen in the main part of this interpretation. Some other, perhaps surprising, Socratic kinships may also emerge.

Despite Kant's words that seem to cut the opposite way, imagination plays a *creative* and *philosophical* role and so perhaps cuts even *more deeply* in the *Critique of Practical Reason* than elsewhere.

Weapons of War

Preliminary Reflections on the Practical in
the *Critique of Pure Reason*

The goal of the book is nothing less than to establish the fidelity of
the interpretation, first propounded by Fichte and Schelling, more
recently and controversially by Heidegger, and advanced by Sallis
within his own more radical interpretive framework,[1] that any judi-
cious reading of Kant's critical philosophy must conclude that imagination is primary. Theirs is the work upon which I proudly build,
extending the thread of this seminal way of interpretation to the *Critique of Practical Reason*.

However, I speak to many audiences besides those already influenced by this interpretive strain. I hope to provide encouragement to
students of Kant who find the prevailing Anglo-American Kant literature puzzling, since it not only fails to treat imagination ade-
quately, but also sometimes fails to treat it at all.[2] I also hope to challenge readers of Kant in that prevailing tradition to take the measure
of this interpretation.[3] Although my orientation is mainly continental, I believe that the rigor of my textual exegesis will amply reward
their time and attention, despite the many hackles it is likely to raise.
Finally, many continental philosophers who hold the *Critique of Pure
Reason* (also the *Critique of Judgment*) in the highest esteem withhold
such esteem from the second critique. I aim to persuade them to

grant that same esteem to the *Critique of Practical Reason,* as I also enter into dialogue with my continental colleagues.[4]

In the Prologue, I showed how imagination occupies the animating center of the *Critique of Pure Reason.* Can the same centrality be exhibited for the *Critique of Practical Reason?* In my view, the answer both is, and must be, a resounding "yes!" Kant consistently insists upon the unity of his entire philosophy and especially upon the consistency between the first two critiques. Further, for a Kantian who is convinced of the unity of the Kantian philosophy,[5] it is incumbent upon me to provide an account of this unity. The goal of this book is to provide precisely such an account. No special interpretive measures, unless close attention to the key passages in the text can be called "special," are required.

I have consciously chosen to avoid recourse to the *Critique of Judgment.* While it may be tempting to exploit the apparently more liberal employment of imagination in this third critique in order to illuminate those more obscure regions of the *Critique of Practical Reason* from which imagination seems most expressly excluded, this would defeat the principal goal of this work, which is to exhibit imagination even and especially where it seems to be entirely absent and to do so in terms internal to the work.[6] However, the task of exposing imagination's work beneath the surface of Kant's moral philosophy is much more difficult given Kant's almost total silence concerning it. This silence is especially noteworthy in the *Critique of Practical Reason,* for this work (together with the *Foundations of the Metaphysics of Morals*[7]) constitutes the pure part upon which the whole of the practical philosophy rests.

Heidegger, whose *Kant and the Problem of Metaphysics* argued for imagination's being the "unknown" root of understanding and sensibility in the first edition of the *Critique of Pure Reason,* also argued (albeit briefly) for imagination's central role in the *Critique of Practical Reason.* There, he claims that "the origin of practical reason can be understood from transcendental imagination," and presents duty and action as imagination's original unifying of the "self-subjecting immediate giving of the law (pure spontaneity) and the free pregiving-to-oneself" of the law (pure receptivity) and "the free self-imposition of the moral law" (spontaneity),[8] a unification that—I say—has always already taken place.

Heidegger says that Kant "recoiled" from the radicality of the view that imagination is the "unknown root" and presented a tamer version in the B edition, in which understanding is given ascendancy.[9] This Heideggerian provocation has been of inestimable value to me. However, I take issue with this view elsewhere, arguing that in §24 of the B edition imagination sustains equal force when measured against its more obvious ascendancy in the A edition.[10] However, Heidegger's general observation leads to a crucial element in my Kant interpretation, an element exposed with thoroughgoing clarity and justice in Sallis's *Spacings—of Reason and Imagination*. Kant's texts are as far as possible from being doctrinal. Rather, they are *heterogeneous*, with key internal elements working in opposition to one another. The most obvious is the early declaration that reason is so perfect a unity that it can answer every question put to it, and the recognition of the antinomies, which sets reason at odds with itself.[11]

The heterogeneity that both allows for and governs this interpretation is rooted precisely in Heidegger's observation that, if it does not hold for the B Deduction, it nevertheless exposes the fundamental tension and opposition between a critique of pure reason under the title of (in Kant's own words) an "Analytic of the Pure Understanding" and a critique of pure reason driven by (again in Kant's own words) "synthesis, the mere result of imagination." I maintain that like Plato, Kant is engaged in the most fundamental philosophical dialogue, only this dialogue works as both surface and depth in his texts.

But once again my goal is modest, namely to get Kant right. However, given Kant's aforementioned reticence on imagination in his writings on pure moral philosophy, the means must be more ambitious. Before I begin my delineation of the interpretive tools I must employ in order to reach the goal, it is worthwhile to recall Kant's own reminder on wholeness in philosophy, first articulated in the "Architectonic of Pure Reason" of the *Critique of Pure Reason* and reiterated forcefully in the *Critique of Practical Reason*. While it is necessary, in order to determine the origin, contents, and limits of a particular faculty of the human mind, to delineate its parts as precisely as possible, it is "more philosophical and architectonic" to grasp correctly "the idea of the whole, and then to see the parts in all their interrelations" (V, 10). Kant calls this latter, "second stage" the "synoptic view, which is a synthetic return to that which is given only analytically" (V, 10). This recalls the remark at A97: "to such synopsis a synthesis must always correspond."[12] Here, a twofold synthesis presents itself: (1) the synthesis required in order to attain the idea of a systematic whole itself and (2) the synthesis of the parts into a whole. This twofold synthesis should be kept in mind in all that follows.

In the *Critique of Pure Reason*, the most apparently simple perceptions as well as the most innocuous-seeming tautologies, not to mention the most pregnant principles as well as the most fruitful empirical judgments, conceal a synthesis of imagination, a synthesis that has always already taken place. By means of sensation alone, no determination of objects is possible. This is clear. But further, by means of understanding, i.e., by means of concepts alone, not only is it the case that not one single object can be determined. Further, not one predicate can be attached to any subject without imagination, even though imagination is nowhere to be discerned. In other words, the interpretation there as well as here presupposes a unified view of synthesis, namely that it is always the work of imagination. The governing text, already cited in both the Prologue and Introduction above, is from the *Critique of Pure Reason:* "Synthesis in general (*überhaupt*) as we shall hereafter see, is the result of the power of imagination, a blind but indispensable function of the soul, without which we would have no knowledge whatsoever, but of which we are scarcely ever conscious" (A78, B103). Where Kant departs from this way of speaking of synthesis, he departs not only from his most clearly stated view of synthesis, but also from his most original and challenging insight.

As will be shown, imagination conceals its workings just as deeply in the *Critique of Practical Reason* and the *Foundations of the Metaphysics of Morals* as it does on occasion in the *Critique of Pure Reason*, but it is just as fully and abidingly present. Since the *Foundations* concerns itself primarily with the clarification of the concept of duty and not with the systematic issues discussed above, the interpretation will address itself to the *Critique*, drawing upon the *Foundations* when its material will prove helpful.

To provide a brief glimpse ahead, the exposure of imagination at the heart of Kant's practical philosophy may serve to make this philosophy—too often characterized as joyless and as at least partially unsuited to our nature—appear in a friendlier light. This is not to say that it is philosophy's task to make matters easier or more palatable. But to be "friendly," φίλιον, belongs, after all, to philosophy's first name. It is my hope that the reader will find Kant to be a much better, more interesting, and more engaging friend than might have been supposed at first.

* * *

At the outset of the Transcendental Doctrine of Method of the *Critique of Pure Reason*, Kant employs the metaphorics of architecture to describe the possibilities remaining for human habitation, given the elements and their limits at our disposal: not a tower reaching to the heavens, but a humbler "dwelling house commodious enough for our business on the level of experience, and just sufficiently high to allow of our overlooking it" (A707, B735). The Doctrine of Method will provide the plan that would fashion such a building in accord with the nature of the available materials. This building would also be constructed "according to the measure of our need" (*unserem Bedürfniß angemessen ist*) (A707, B735).

Expressed in more logical language, the Doctrine of Method is "the determination of the formal conditions of the complete system of pure reason" (A708, B736). But these formal conditions are not disclosed at all through logic. They become manifest through the recognition of reason's own limits and through the field of possibility opened up by virtue of this recognition. The logical language is always in service to human life for Kant, always at the disposal of we architects who must fashion—like the guardians of Plato's *Republic*—houses appropriate for our natures.

However, in order to erect such a building, conditions must be peaceful on the ground where the building will sit. The ground cannot be the site of ongoing battles. The title to the ground upon which it is to be erected must be cleared and free of all counterclaims. Only in this way can both the architect and the dweller, who are one and the same person, be confident that the house under construction is safe from attack. Accordingly, Kant includes a section in the midst of the Doctrine of Method governed by the metaphorics of *war*. In order to secure the required peace, reason must first fight and—at least for all *practical* purposes—vanquish its enemies. The weapons with which it fights are *hypotheses*. "For our complete equipment we require among other things the *hypotheses* of pure reason" (A778, B806).

In a striking passage from the "Discipline of Pure Reason," Section 3, a discussion of the formation of hypotheses moves quite close to declaring that imagination has the power not only to fashion hypotheses but also to *create the practical realm itself*, albeit "under the strict oversight of reason" (which can create nothing):

> If the imagination (*Einbildungskraft*) is not to rave (*schwärmen*) but to *create* (*dichten*) under the strict oversight (*Aufsicht*) of reason, there must always previously be something that is completely certain and not invented (*erdichtet*) or a mere opinion, and that is the *possibility* of the object itself. (A769–70, B797–98)

The hypotheses so created by imagination have the ideas of reason as their matter: (1) the freedom of the will, (2) the immortality of the soul, and (3) the existence of God. None of them admits to the slightest possibility of proof or probability. Kant makes it absolutely clear that in a contest between the disputant who hypothesizes the reality of the ideas and those who deny their reality, neither side can make the least headway against the other. No proposition can be based upon them either way: "[T]hey may not be employed in any dogmatic, but only in polemical fashion" (A776, B804). The war they undertake with one another is an unavoidable one, rooted in the nature of reason itself. "Hypotheses are therefore, in the domain of pure reason, permissible only as weapons of war, and only for the purpose of defending a right, not in order to establish it" (A777,

B806). However, the defense provided by hypotheses based upon the hypothesized reality of the ideas is essential to both the clearing out of potential hindrances and the ongoing protection of the practical realm itself. They are a very strange kind of weapon. Kant calls them "leaden (*bleirne*) weapons, since they are not steeled by any law of experience" (A778, B806), yet the defense they mount is impregnable.

Here, the likeness of Kantian insight to Socratic ignorance, its ancient kin, could not be stronger. In the *Apology*, Socrates' defense consisted of his claim that he knew nothing worth knowing. Any advantage that he might enjoy in comparison with others rested upon his recognition that, with respect to concerns of real importance to human beings, he knew that he knew nothing (see esp. 22e–23b). Thus others who supposed they had knowledge of such significant matters but did not were worse off than him.

Echoes of Socratic ignorance resonate in the Kantian treatment of the ideas of reason and the hypotheses that are fashioned from them. With respect to the supersensible realm, no one knows anything. Therefore, any claim to knowledge is *a fortiori* not to be credited. Such a claim can be rebuffed by any counterclaim, which will be equally problematic but which will serve sufficiently to thwart the original claim entirely.

Consider, for example, that one claimant maintains that it is illicit "to suppose that a creature [you or I] whose life has first begun in circumstances so trivial and our freedom so entirely given over to these circumstances should have an existence that extends to all eternity" (A779, B807). As an answer, one can respond with equal justice—that is to say, out of the same thoroughgoing ignorance of ultimate matters—that "all life is, strictly speaking, intelligible only, and neither begins in birth nor ends in death" (A780, B808). From the standpoint of knowledge, neither position has the slightest merit.

For the Kantian text just as in the Platonic one, acts of language (*logos*) are the weapons. In the *Phaedrus*, Socrates and Phaedrus consider an exchange in which neither speaker knew what a horse was, but that one knew that the other supposed that a horse was a donkey. The first speaker then proceeded to praise the donkey by ascribing every equine quality he had heard of to "the animal with the longest ears." Phaedrus agrees that such an exchange would be "most ridiculous of all" (260b–c). The possible exchanges within theoretical reason that Kant relates in this section may even surpass their Platonic ancestor in preposterousness: in the *Phaedrus,* neither call nor response come into any contact with their subject matter; in the Kantian supersensible claims, there are in principle neither horses nor donkeys to which one could appeal at all.

Further aspects of the Platonic kinship here are even more striking. Just as the absence of knowledge spurs the Socratic search for the *logoi* that would guide a good life, for Kant the radical impossibility of establishing claims of supersensible knowledge opens up a different realm in which reason can likewise direct one to a good life for a human being:

> This equality of fortune [in the ventures of] human reason does not, in speculative modes of knowledge, favor either of the two parties, and it is consequently the fitting battle-ground for their never-ending feuds. But as will be shown, reason has, in respect to its *practical* employment, the right to postulate what in the field of speculation it can have no right to assume without sufficient proof. (A776, B804)

While the hypotheses as weapons of war must be deployed against the external enemies of morality, their primary use is against those internal enemies, so that the dialectical nature of our own speculative reason rises into relief. The "attacks" can surely be presented as having an external origin, much as Glaucon and Adiemantus ascribe such an origin to their doubts about leading a just life in Plato's *Republic,* Book II. They are influenced by the general public reputation of justice as drudgery. In the eyes of the public (*hoi polloi,* "the many"), doing justice is a compromise between doing perfect injustice without suffering consequences (this is best of all) and suffering perfect injustice without means of redress (this is worst of all). Further, it is better to *appear* just than to *be* just. They ask to hear Socrates praise justice for its own sake and for the benefits it brings, overturning public opinion. It is clear, however, that the battleground is within their own souls.

In analogous fashion, the Theses and Antitheses in the Antinomies that represent the two aforementioned "contestants of the supersensible" are ascribed to an irreconcilable division within reason itself. Most fundamentally, they are not accounts of views held by two different persons (although each of the views can be ascribed to holders of their respective philosophical positions). Therefore, while the weapons of war must be deployed in defense against any external enemy who might attempt to threaten the integrity of the practical sphere with some piece of bogus knowledge, this defense requires no great effort. Their primary use is against those internal enemies, so that the dialectical nature of our own speculative reason becomes integral to our self-knowledge. In this way, the futility of the inner war of theoretical reason with itself becomes clear to us so that we humans may make the appropriate peace in the only way we can, i.e., in the practical realm. In my view, this is one of the best ways to interpret Kant's often cited comment in the Preface to the B edition: "I have therefore found it necessary to deny *knowledge* in order to make room for *belief (Glaube)*" (Bxxx).

However, there is an overflow from Kant's language in this section that suggests a direction far bolder even than the fashioning of hypotheses as defensive weapons. In the passage cited above, he spoke of the power of imagination to "create (*dichten*) under the strict oversight of reason." *Dichten* has many meanings, most often associated with creative work such as poetry or composition, always involving invention of some kind. Reading *dichten* in this context most narrowly, I read it as saying that imagination "creates" the hypotheses that will defend the practical realm from its enemies. Reason's "oversight" consists in its "sight" of the ideas, and in its critical restriction of the ideas to their regulative employment. Imagination, then, guided by the ideas of reason, fashions synthetic judgments that incorporate the ideas such that they become expressed as hypotheses. The ideas are "something not invented or a mere opinion." They, together with their regulative restriction, are the anchors that keep imagination's creation within proper bounds.

However, an even more ambitious reading emerges upon further reflection. What are the ideas, most notably the idea of freedom? They are the *sources of the practical realm itself*! By themselves, they are mere inert expressions of the pure concepts of the understanding extended beyond any possible experience to the absolute totality that lies beyond any possibility of knowledge. But as so extended and used, the creation of hypotheses as weapons of war under the oversight of reason outstrips the powerful defense it provides. This creation is at once *the creation of the idea of the practical realm itself.* This realm surely awaits much development and much ordering. Kant indicates a key step belonging to such ordering here in his suggestion that in the practical realm, one can postulate as real what cannot be proven theoretically. This postulation will itself involve imagination's creation under the oversight of reason. The idea of freedom will move to the center of this ordering, for reasons that will soon become manifest. But there can be no fashioning of a practical realm in general without both envisioning this realm and protecting it at the same time. The architect has to have both a plan and safe ground upon which to proceed building.

As will be shown in what follows, the entire edifice of reason is erected by imagination in service to the measure of human need as expressed at the opening of the Doctrine of Method. Strictly speaking, although the ground for practical philosophy is protected by a hypothesis, this ground is not itself a weapon of war. On the contrary, it is depicted as an area within which the clamors that may occur in human desire can be quieted. It serves as a location where one can bring one's humanity into harmony with itself and with the whole of its activities out of its various discords. The *Critique of Pure Reason* in its Methodology traces out the possibility and the general contours of a plan to erect an appropriate human edifice. To direct our powers suitably and to prevent us from going astray in this architectural enterprise, a *Critique of Practical Reason* is needed to complement its predecessor.

"PREFACE" AND "INTRODUCTION"

I

The first sentence of the third paragraph of the Preface (broken into three separate sentences in Beck's translation) is no mere casual preliminary. Rather, it is the laying out of the problematic of both the *Critique of Practical Reason* itself and of its relation to the entire system of reason. It reads:

> The concept of freedom, insofar as its reality (*Realität*) is proved by an apodictic law of practical reason, constitutes the *keystone* of the whole edifice of a system of pure reason, even of speculative reason, and all other concepts (those of God and immortality) which remain as mere ideas without support in speculative reason now attach themselves to freedom and, with it and through it, receive firmness (*Bestand*) and objective reality (*Realität*), i.e., their *possibility* is *proven* through the fact that (*dadurch*) freedom is actual (*wirklich*); because this idea reveals itself through the moral law." (V, 4)

I now ask a series of questions about this startling sentence.

(1) Whence the idea of freedom? Its origin, in terms of the delineation of the elements (the parts), is presented in the Third Antinomy of the Transcendental Dialectic of the *Critique of Pure Reason*. It issues from the extension of the concept of causality to the unconditioned. Kant defines it in that context as "unconditioned causality" (A419, B447). This concept belongs to both the thesis (affirmatively) and the antithesis (negatively), each of which is a synthetic *a priori* judgment. Both synthetic *a priori* judgments are the work of imagination. The extension itself is also the work of imagination.

As John Sallis pointed out so clearly in the notion upon which *The Gathering of Reason* turned,[13] imagination has the twofold role of (1) synthesizing, but also of (2) image-making. Since no single image can be constructed following the rule presented by both the judgment of the thesis and that of the antithesis, no knowledge regarding either of them is possible.[14] Consider a hypothetical case under the Third Antinomy, in which I provide truthful testimony where such testimony could make me the object of anger and rebuke. My action is clearly in accord with the moral law, but this is not necessarily the case with respect to the ground of my action, which may include a measure of self-love (more on this later). Since the categories have no direct images but rather the appearances themselves stand in for images,[15] there is no way to determine whether two conjoined events, e.g., (a) my truthful representation upon being required to give testimony and (b) my truthful compliance, occurred only through natural (i.e., conditioned) causality or through freedom (ultimately) as well.

Thus, not only has the concept of freedom been generated by imagination, and not only are both thetic and antithetic judgments formed by imagination, it further follows that imagination *sets the measure* for this antinomy, leaves its outcome indeterminate, and so allows for freedom's *not being ruled out* of the world.

As a result of imagination's generation and limiting of the concept of freedom, the epistemological status of freedom is very narrowly circumscribed in the *Critique of Pure Reason*. On freedom's behalf, Kant does not even claim that he has proven its possibility. "What we have alone been able to show, is that this antinomy rests on an illusion (*Schein*) [namely that the world is an object of experience], and that causality through freedom is at least *not incompatible* with nature" (A558, B586).

(2) However, as has already been indicated, freedom's character is presented by Kant, at least in part, in a positive way: it is *spontaneous*, and it is *intelligible*. How is this so? That is, what justifies the move (made quite early in Kant's discussion) from the mere non-non-compatibility of freedom and necessity to freedom's spontaneity and intelligibility? Once again, it is a case of imagination running up against its own limits: "But since in this way [i.e., proceeding backward endlessly from a conditioned to its condition (its cause) and so seeking the 'sum total of the merely natural'] no absolute totality of conditions determining causal relations can be obtained, *reason creates for itself (schafft sich) the idea of a spontaneity* that can begin to act of itself, without needing to be determined to action by an antecedent cause in accordance with the law of causality" (A533, B562, emphasis mine). This inability of imagination to complete the empirical regress leaves room for a spontaneous, intelligible causality to be posited as possible.[16]

However, in the strict sense, reason *creates nothing*. Although at various times Kant calls reason "the *faculty of principles*" (A299, B356, emphasis in original), it is also called the faculty of mediate inference (with the appropriate critical adjustments) (A303–304, B360–

61). Reason further makes demands for a synthesis such that "*if the conditioned is given, the entire sum of conditions, and consequently the absolutely unconditioned . . . is also given*" (A409, B436, emphasis in original). Kant also speaks in more appropriately measured tones: "Reason really generates no concepts (*die Vernunft eigentlich gar keine Begriffe erzeuge*) (A409, B435). Imagination does the "creating," either by extending reason's concepts by means of the aforementioned synthesis or by fashioning artworks without the aid of concepts at all.[17] With reason understood in its narrower senses as faculty of mediate inference and as faculty of principles, it engages in no creation at all. *Imagination* effects the synthesis of the categories and pure intuition that yields the principles (*Grundsätze*) of the pure understanding (so called because they concern the relation of concepts to experience). Imagination also extends these into principles of another kind (*Principien*), thereby enabling the latter to ascend to the unconditioned, where, as maxims, they can bring unity to the manifold of the understanding (see A670–71, B698–99).[18] For Kant, then, the function of our faculty of thought is not creation, but the mere provision of unity to our fragmented intuition. Only the divine being (itself a pure image) creates its object in the very act of knowing it, i.e., has intellectual intuition. Our intuition is derivative, and our thought "always involves limitations" (see B71–72). The closest that the human mind comes to creation in the realm of *knowledge*[19] is in geometry, where, as pure science of space, the concept gives the rule for its own construction in intuition. But this cannot serve as a direct analogue in the treatment of freedom: freedom can be brought to no image whatsoever.

However, geometry can provide an indirect analogy. For the objects of geometry are not the drawn objects on the page, which are sensuous images of the concept, but their imagination-produced schemata that exist "nowhere but in thought" (A141, B180). The drawn triangle for a Euclidean proof concerning all triangles, for example, is always overdetermined when compared with the concept "triangle": the lines of the triangle on the page have width; the triangle is also either isosceles, equilateral, or scalene. The general schema of the triangle is no image at all, but "a rule for the synthesis of imagination, in respect to figures in space" (A140, B180).

In this very limited sense, by exhibiting concepts in intuition in accord with a rule, we create our own objects in the act of knowing them. But these objects, the objects of geometry, are *ideal* and not real. Further, their exhibition in intuition requires that they exceed the concept, that (to speak in a logical mode) they contain predicates other than those already contained in the concept.

How can this be applied to the concept of freedom? Kant seems to say that freedom is created due to a lack, a certain failure, perhaps even a certain frustration, that issues from the effort to determine the nature and scope of the concept of causality. The concept "Euclidean triangle" is a universal concept, and so includes all possible triangles under it. But the restriction of geometry to intuition (space) means that, by definition, triangles are (ideal) objects of (pure) sensation.[20] But this restriction is absent in the concept of causality (as it is in all three categories of relation), which is a pure concept of *understanding*, and so occurs on the side of spontaneity.

Liberated from this sensible condition, reason strives for absolute totality in the causal series. But its synthesizing image-making dark faculty called imagination simply cannot deliver absolute totality. Bound to temporal finite experience, imagination must always be able to imagine another cause before the last one discovered in the temporal series. What about this "always having to imagine another cause"? In one sense, this imagining is bound to the principle of causality of the Analytic, namely that appearances are one and all subject to its law. So the imagined cause must be another appearance, i.e., must have a receptive (sensuous) element. However, there is an "empty space" in our causal knowledge that is not present in our geometrical knowledge. This is the case because (a) all our geometrical knowledge refers back to fundamental concepts that function as rules for the construction of all geometrical objects, while our causal knowledge is capable of no such reference, and (b) no causal series can be regarded as absolutely complete the way a geometrical proof can be so regarded.

While the law of causality commands that nothing other than another appearance can extend and so enter *into* the series, it does not and cannot command that a natural cause is the only possible cause *of* the series. The only requirement that attaches to the concept of causality is that everything that happens has a (natural) cause, i.e., follows according to a rule.[21] The causal law does not rule out another source of another rule, namely an *intelligible* source: reason or, more strictly speaking, understanding that first gives rise to the concept of causality itself, now freed from its bond to intuition and so extended to the unconditioned.

While Kant presented the generation of the concept of freedom relatively late in the *Critique of Pure Reason,* it is crucial to note that freedom itself *has no antecedent.* It is the product of no inference. It is governed by no principle. Given the generally uncreative nature of reason, there is only one way to account for Kant's claim that reason has created this concept: if reason is regarded not merely in terms of one of its manifestations but as the entire higher faculty, then it includes *imagination* as its creative element. Freedom is the pure product of imagination, extending itself out of nowhere into the gap of our causal knowledge. Once again, from the standpoint of theoretical reason we do not know whether freedom is possible in reality. If it is, however, one may strongly suspect that it is both ideal and that it leads to knowledge (of a kind) beyond its mere concept, i.e., that it is in some way analogous to our geometrical knowledge.

(3) How can the *reality* of freedom be proven from an apodictic law of practical reason? The *Critique of Practical Reason* presupposes the material presented in the *Foundations of the Metaphysics of Morals,* in which Kant claims that "all moral philosophy rests entirely upon its pure part" (IV, 389). Thus, a brief excursion through key issues in that work will serve well here. The distinctions Kant makes between actions contrary to duty, actions done in accordance with duty, and those actions that qualify as moral by virtue of their being done from duty are well-known even to the most recalcitrant undergraduates. For the *Critique,* the *Foundations* provides the account of the nature of lawfulness peculiar to practical reason.

The pre-eminent good that is called moral does not, strictly speaking, reside in any particular law as the determining ground of the will. Rather, it resides in what Kant calls "nothing other than *the representation (Vorstellung) of the law* in itself, *which clearly (freilich) takes place only in rational beings*" (IV, 401, emphasis in original). This law, the categorical imperative, reads, "So act that the maxim of your will could always hold (*gelten könne*) at the same time as a principle establishing universal law." It is not presented until §7 in the *Critique of Practical Reason*.

In the *Foundations*, however, Kant already has called attention to the synthetic *a priori* character[22] of the judgment in which the law is expressed and to the difficulties involved in the establishment of the possibility of such judgments insofar as they relate to *action*. In the *Critique of Practical Reason*, Kant is concerned with establishing the synthetic *a priori* character of the *law itself*. In fact, these are two simultaneous syntheses, separable only in speech. In a key footnote in the *Foundations*, he delineates the elements of the former synthesis:

> I connect (*verknüpfe*) the action with the will without a presupposed condition from any inclination *a priori*, therefore necessarily (although not objectively, i.e., under an idea of reason that would have [*hätte*] complete power over all subjective motives [*Bewegursachen*]). The latter is therefore a practical proposition that does not derive the willing of an action analytically from another willing that has already been presupposed (because we do not have such a perfect will), but rather connects (*verknüpft*) it immediately with the concept of the will of a rational being as something that is not contained in the willing.[23] (IV, 420n)

Once again, this synthesis has always already taken place. The two elements already synthesized are (1) the action and (2) the pure will. Imagination has already done its work, again out of view. The categorical imperative serves as the bridge between the two elements. But this very bridge, which is called "the fundamental law of practical reason" in §7 of the *Critique of Practical Reason*, is itself a synthetic *a priori* proposition. So both the connection of the action and the pure will and the bridge that makes this connection possible are *a priori* syntheses.

Kant selects an apt adjectival phrase for this state of affairs, in which the consciousness of this law occurs without any antecedent and in which a synthetic *a priori* proposition "forces itself upon us based on no pure or empirical intuition." He calls it "strange enough (*befremdlich genug*)." Strange enough that a critique of reason depends for its very possibility on imagination, the faculty that hides itself and so stands in tension with the self-transparency that reason is supposed to have. Kant writes, "In this field nothing can escape us. What reason produces entirely out of itself cannot be concealed" (Axx). How strange, how utterly *foreign*, that the very source of this *self*-production to itself is hidden from view in reason's most important use!

What is the epistemological status of the consciousness of this law? It is "the unique fact of pure reason" (V, 31). But where do "facts" fit into the Kantian delineation of elements? They are neither intelligible nor sensible, although the law has an intelligible source while the will's actions occur in the domain of sense. If the working of imagination, spoken of as concealed in the depths of the human soul in the *Critique of Pure Reason*, was dark and unconscious, this darkness and unconsciousness is even more remarkable here. For it produces not merely a connection of concepts and intuitions that are given through the nature of our minds, but a *fact* that has always already arisen out of nowhere! Further, it is a *pure* fact, dwelling between the intelligible and sensible regions, determining the will to act according to a certain kind of maxim and no other.

This "sole fact of reason," nowhere to be found in Kant's epistemological nomenclature, is a *pure image*, as is freedom, its reciprocal. This phrase should raise no eyebrows: Kant consistently maintained that we have no knowledge of originals of any kind. In the third section of the *Foundations*, entitled "Transition from the Metaphysics of Morals to the Critical Examination of Pure Practical Reason," Kant prepares both for this fact and this strangeness. What can we *know* through reason regarding the practical realm? "[R]eason would overstep all its bounds if it undertook to *explain* how pure reason could be practical, which is the same as explaining *how freedom is possible*" (IV, 458–59, emphases in original). The possibility of a categorical imperative can be explained by recourse to the presupposition of freedom, but the explanation of this presupposition is—once again—impossible (IV, 461).

So the concluding sentence of the *Foundations* comes as no surprise: "We do not indeed conceive the practical unconditional necessity of the moral law, but we conceive its *inconceivability,* which is all that can be reasonably (*billigermassen*) demanded of a philosophy that in its principles strives to reach the limits of human reason" (463). The "practical unconditional necessity of the moral law," in a word its *apodicticity,* cannot be a concept, and it cannot be an intuition. It is another image dwelling at the heart of pure practical reason. Thus, the reality of freedom, together with the apodictic law that proves this reality, belongs to a *play of images.* By "play," no randomness is implied, any more than playing chess, for example, is random. This play is a lawful play. But it cannot be denied that images are at play at the key stations in the Kantian text.

In *The Gathering of Reason,* John Sallis concludes his interpretation of the *Critique of Pure Reason* with this seminal insight into the nature of imaging in the Kantian text:

> an image is by definition attached to a dyadic structure—that is, it is an image *of* something, *even if* that of which it is an image cannot be declared an ultimate intelligible, an original beyond all imaging, a final security aloof from the play. . . . Nothing escapes the play; one finds everywhere only the play of imaging, the play of indeterminate dyads. In turning toward images one is, in the end, turned toward the play of imaging.[24]

For Kant, even *reality* occurs as the product of imagination, namely as imagination's generating the schema as "the quantity of something as it fills time" (A143, B183). There seems to be, however, a marked difference between the image-play in which the reality of freedom occurs and the image-play in which the category of reality in the *Critique of Pure Reason* occurs. The latter, expressed in the principle "all appearances are intensive magnitudes," achieves its connection to intuition by means of its aforementioned schema. Thus, "reality" in the context of theoretical knowledge requires a receptive element and occurs as the interplay of spontaneity and receptivity. The reality of freedom, however, has no receptive component whatsoever. It occurs within the interplay of spontaneity itself, namely in terms of pure laws on the one hand and unconditioned causality on the other. And we have no knowledge of either.

Nevertheless, there is a kinship that, despite the difference, reflects back upon the systematic structure of the critical philosophy. The Principles of the Pure Understanding that include the category of Reality in the *Critique of Pure Reason* are called "Anticipations of Perception." In the Anticipations, something that can be given only through sensation, namely the intensity of an appearance at any moment in time, is projected independently of sensation. Their principle (again, that all appearances are intensive magnitudes, i.e., admit of a degree) determines not one single object. Nevertheless, just as the principle of the Axioms of Intuition does, the principle of the Anticipations sets out the field of experience together with the limits of that field upon which anything can appear. According to the Axioms, every appearance must have an extensive magnitude; according to the Anticipations, every appearance must have an intensive magnitude or degree, namely that the intensity of the appearance at any moment in time has a quantity greater than zero and less than one.

Analogously, the moral law anticipates *maxims* that govern action in the world of sense in an analogous way, namely independently of any sensation and of any rule in which empirical content is present. No particular maxim is determined by this law, which sets out the field of maxims that can qualify as moral. However, unlike the Anticipations, which set out the field for all appearances, the moral law sets out the field for only those maxims by which all rational beings *ought* to govern her or his actions. There are other possible maxims as well that we may choose, maxims that fail the test of the "ought."

In the language of the Kantian text, our ability to choose maxims that enable us to rule ourselves from a law (i.e., an imperative issuing from our rational selves in the face of other imperatives, i.e., exercise our *autonomy*) establishes the reality of freedom. In other words, by means of our acting from the moral law, we no longer allow ourselves to be determined by the causality of the world of sense but enter an intelligible world in which we legislate for ourselves from ourselves—a world in which freedom is the keystone.

In the language that speaks from the depths of the same text, the human being finds herself or himself at play within the ever-ongoing interplay of sensible and intelligible. Within this interplay, competing claims of goodness and happiness, neither of which can ever be fully satisfied, extend themselves toward human beings from within their humanity. Happiness is vague and ever-shifting: "what is to bring true, lasting advantage to our whole existence is veiled in impenetrable darkness" (V, 36). But duty, although said by contrast here to be "plain of itself to everyone (*bietet sich jedermannn von selbst dar*)," is itself veiled in its own way: "it is in fact completely impossible by experience to discern with complete certainty a single case in which the maxim of an action . . . rested solely on moral grounds" (IV, 407).

Although we humans are neither clever enough to secure abiding happiness nor honorable enough to secure an abiding moral stance, though granted enticing glimpses of both this happiness and that morality, the entire worth of the human being is seen by Kant in terms of the victory of duty. While this victory cannot have any specifically religious motive, Kant does say that "*religion is the recognition (Erkenntnis) of duties as divine commands, not as sanctions, i.e., arbitrary accidental orders of an alien will for itself*, but rather as essential *laws* of each free will for itself" (V, 129). One such command is to treat humanity, in ourselves and in others, always as an end and never as a means only (IV, 429).[25] But given the play of forces that shape the struggle to which the human being is handed over, and the limited means given with which to undertake that struggle, there is a depth to that notion of humanity that might best be articulated in the words, cited by Sallis at the end of *The Gathering of Reason*, of the Athenian Stranger in Plato's *Laws*, who called man (at least his best part) "a plaything of the gods."[26]

Thus, in the language of the Kantian text, the nature of the moral law both as demonstrably certain (it is the form of any imperative) and as admitting of the possibility of its *not* being employed for maxim selection, establishes the reality of freedom: if freedom were not real and a real ground of (anticipated) action in terms of maxims, the moral law would not be a moral law, i.e., a law involving an *ought*. In the language of imagination, freedom is nothing other than the *human being at play within the image play to which he is given over*. The determination of the moral sphere on the surface of the text conceals the mapping of this playground.

In order to provide a preliminary glimpse into the justice of this interpretation, and also to expose the injustice of interpreting Kant's ethics as excessively austere and as entailing great seriousness, I turn briefly to the section on "Self-Mastery" from Kant's *Lectures on Ethics*. It would seem, in this section, that imagination is cast as the enemy of moral action, and man is characterized as much more than a plaything:

> If he does not have himself under control, his imagination (*Imagination*) has free play; he cannot discipline himself, but is carried away by it, according to the laws of association, since he willingly yields to the senses; if he cannot restrain himself, he becomes their plaything (*Spiel*).[27] Autocracy should consist, then, in a man's banishing his imaginings from his mind, so that imagination (*Imagination*[28]) does not work its spell (*Zauberspiel*) of presenting objects that are unobtainable.[29]

But the excision of imagination entails the excision of the moral law and with it the excision of the possibility of self-mastery, as well as the possibility of any knowledge (including self-knowledge) at all. This is why Kant offers a solution out of a kind of desperation. Since the allure of the senses and the associations formed by reproductive imagination cannot be excised, we must somehow seduce ourselves away from its pernicious influence:

> With regard to the senses in general, since they dupe and also outwit (*überlisten*) the understanding, *we can do nothing else but outwit them in turn,* by trying to furnish the mind with another form of sustenance than that offered by the senses, and seeking to occupy it with idealistic pleasures (*Idealistische Vergnügen*) that belong to all beautiful sciences.[30] (27: 364–65, emphasis mine)

This *self-seduction* is another name for our freedom. The moral law constrains us to master ourselves in the sense that we freely submit our actions to its rule. But here, this self-mastery requires the engagement of *cunning* with *cunning*,[31] in other words the engagement of imagination with itself. Perhaps with hesitation (since the *Lectures on Ethics* are not part of the critical writings proper, and also are a compilation of a student's notes) one can liken this self-engagement of cunning with cunning to the "war" within human reason treated in the Methodology and discussed earlier in this text.

How do "idealistic pleasures" and "beautiful sciences" differ from the "real" pleasures in the world of sense, their tantalizing after-images, and the coarser knowledge associated with our pathological needs? It would be mistaken to say that the former are purely intelligible while the latter are sensuous. There are non-sensuous pathological objects (honor, pride, the admiration of others, intellectual pursuits, for example) and sensuous elements in the most refined knowledge (of plant or animal speciation, for example). The genuine distinction concerns the predominance of *productive* vs. *reproductive imagination,* or in terms of the fundamental Kantian project, it concerns whether we are actively putting our own questions to nature (including those concerning our own nature) or whether we merely receive impressions from without. Even in the *Anthropology,* a work in which the understanding with its seriousness seems to be in ascendancy at the expense of imagination with its playfulness, the language of imagination and play is employed to describe the human condition. "We play often and gladly with the imagination; but the imagination (as fantasy) plays just as often and sometimes very unsuitably with us" (VII, 175).

What about the play that constitutes "idealistic pleasures" and "beautiful sciences"? There is no doubt that both higher forms of knowledge and moral images are concept-determined, the former by theoretical concepts and the latter by practical ones. It is further beyond doubt that understanding is significantly engaged in both, and that its rules govern the play.

But that the human being is at play, of that there can be no doubt. Whether one entertains the differences between Lobachevskian and Riemannian space in order to divert one's thoughts from a lingering salacious impulse experienced earlier that day, or whether one places before oneself an inner narrative of how a Socrates might respond to the hostility of some of his peers in order to quiet his fear and rage, the human being is always drawn toward images—either received, spontaneous, or across the continuum of both.

The reciprocal bond of freedom to the moral law on the surface of the text works itself out in the depths as *the possibility of self-seduction by productive imagination amidst the play of images.*

(4) How does the concept of freedom serve as the *keystone* (*Schluß-stein*) (emphasis in original) of the whole edifice of a system of reason, even of speculative reason?

Although freedom surfaced late and only problematically in the *Critique of Pure Reason,* it must have been present in the depths all along in order to make sense of Kant's claim that it is the keystone of the entire system of reason. Further, the entire Aesthetic and Analytic, in which the elements of theoretical knowledge were disclosed, must be themselves understood in some way as effects of freedom. In this sense, the *Critique of Pure Reason,* a synopsis of which yields (1) the nature of reason's own elements, (2) the limits within which these elements may be properly deployed, and (3) the dangers that lurk in the absence of such critique, is itself a moral act. And since to every synopsis a synthesis must correspond, the entire first critique is at once an act of imagination.

Kant says it is the *concept* of freedom that constitutes the keystone of the entire system. A concept, for Kant, is a rule for the synthesis of a manifold. The core concept here, once again, is *causality*, spontaneous, intelligible causality, causality without antecedent—at least without antecedent in time. The "rule" by means of which this concept rules is a law that we give to ourselves.

In his often cited footnote, Kant calls freedom the *ratio essendi* of the moral law, and the moral law the *ratio cognoscendi* of freedom (V, 4n). However, properly speaking we humans do not *cognize* freedom. We merely infer it from the law in which it is found already embedded. And properly speaking the moral law is not a law. Kant vacillates between calling the moral law (a) a law, (b) the mere form of a law, (c) "mere legislative form of maxims," or (d) "the mere form of giving universal law."[32] Thus freedom is thought through a proposition (the categorical imperative) which resides at the cusp of lawfulness and the mere form of lawfulness. The proposition that ought to govern all practical maxim-formation discloses freedom as noumenal causality. Note that there is *no contact whatsoever* with intuition, pure or empirical, in any of this.[33]

However, following the matters at issue with the same rigor as he did in the *Critique of Pure Reason*, Kant bridges the gap between noumenal and phenomenal causality by noting that the reciprocal relation of freedom and the moral law, and its placement at the heart of the system of reason, does not issue from reason except insofar as reason finds itself *in need* (*Bedürfnis*). The movement from freedom as mere possibility in the *Critique of Pure Reason* to the assertoric reality of freedom in the *Critique of Practical Reason* is a *non sequitur* if regarded as a movement from a premise to its conclusion in formal logic. Formal logic, however, is regioned off mostly to the margins by Kant. Its only function is to rule out self-contradictions. *Need* empowers the transition from the theoretical possibility to the practical actuality of freedom.

How to understand this need? In the Preface, Kant does present it in a logical guise, namely as a necessary presupposition not only for the completion of reason's theoretical task, but as "a need, *with the status of a law*, to assume that without which an aim cannot be achieved which one ought to place invariably with respect to all one's actions and non-actions (*Thuns und Lassens*)" (V, 5). But in both critiques, the deep source from which this logical need surfaces is the fragmented, finite nature of man.

In the *Critique of Pure Reason*, our sensibility and our understanding are characterized as heterogeneous. Our fragmented intuition *needs* the synthesis of imagination and the unity provided by the categories, which, in the principles, make experience possible. In the *Critique of Practical Reason*, Kant addresses our heterogeneous faculties of desire (*Begehrungsvermögen*), one of which is pathologically determined and oriented toward happiness, the other of which is rationally determined and oriented toward goodness. The former *needs* the latter in order that the ultimate aims of humanity, both theoretical and practical, be fulfilled.

The nature of reason itself mitigates some of the need on the side of theory. Theoretical reason has the schemata at its disposal to connect its categories to sensible intuition and so give them sense and significance. The schemata are very "smart" features:[34] by their means the categories automatically determine pure intuition in general and, through them, determine the appearances. The principles of quantity, quality, substance, and causality are normally enough to get most of us humans more or less safely through the shoals of life, even if it would never occur to us to formulate any of them and even if we are somewhat error-prone. But when reason leaves behind the connection to sensibility established by imagination through the schemata, reason comes into a conflict with itself which it cannot resolve but . . . *needs* to. Analogously, on the side of practice the orientation of a human being toward the satisfaction of pathological desire (happiness) is inextricable, but . . . *needs* to be extricated.

The fragmentary nature of intuition, the tendency of reason to transcend its appropriate limits, and the ever-shifting objects of pathological desire all pull against reason's need for unity. For Kant, the assertion of the reality of freedom serves to quell these disturbances and in so doing answer reason's need. This assertion, arising out of nowhere other than the gap between the heterogeneous elements, is again the work of an imagination which effaces itself all the more decisively when it is most at work. Freedom serves as the cornerstone of the system of reason by virtue of its installation into the abyss at the heart of human nature by productive imagination. The moral law, the pure form of giving universal law, is then that pure image of a rationally self-directing will both in its pursuit of truth and in its pursuit of goodness. Freedom serves as a cornerstone, as the main support. It supports both pursuits, and gathers them into a one, into a system. But freedom is not an original; it belongs to the image-play that it serves. On the side of theory, not a single theoretical insight can be derived from it. By its very nature, it exceeds the bounds of theoretical knowledge. On the side of practice, it serves as a measure not of actions, but of maxims. In other words, freedom indeed brings unity, but it does so by leaving the region of its "reign" open to the play of images.

(5) How do the ideas of God and immortality receive firmness and objective reality through the concept of freedom? This question will be treated fully in the discussion of the Dialectic of Practical Reason, but even now it is clear that only by acknowledging the *non-originality* of the ideas of God and immortality can reason save itself from the dynamical antinomies that would keep it divided and that would therefore close off any possibility of achieving the unity it seeks.

The categories of "community" and "substance" in theoretical reason, from which these ideas have their origin, achieve objective reality only insofar as they are at once the conditions in consciousness for the possibility of experience and, by virtue of the connection of consciousness to pure intuition, are the conditions for the possibility of objects of experience (that can appear at all only in space and time). Objective reality is therefore not absolute reality. (The latter could belong only to [unknowable] things in themselves.) Objective reality is established by the referral of all objects of experience to the objective unity of apperception (the "I think"), which must accompany all of my representations and through which the categories are thought. Given the absence of originals even in consciousness together with the determinability by consciousness of pure intuition by means of the schemata of imagination, one must conclude that objective reality is the kind of reality appropriate to a being that is by its very nature *bound to images*.[35]

For theoretical reason, the attempt to break this bond belongs to its nature. When the attempt is made to release the "I think" from its bond to intuition, paralogisms inevitably result: the I that thinks in the subject is divided from the I that is thought through the predicate and so becomes an illicit fourth term.[36] And when loosed from its bond to intuition, the pure concept of the community of substances becomes the idea of the absolute totality of being (God), a concept to which no intuition and therefore no knowledge could possibly correspond. The logical guise of the mistake in this case issues from another concealed conceptual error, namely the belief that existence is a real predicate. Since it is not, all proofs for the existence of God must fail since they all rest upon the ontological proof that presupposes this mistaken belief.[37]

Imagination in Kant's *Critique of Practical Reason*

The logical guise of Kant's criticisms can be represented instead in terms of imagination's more fundamental twofold functioning: the arguments are syntheses and so they are acts of imagination, but they are syntheses that arrest the image play. Neither an image of the soul nor one of God has emerged from the effort to fashion one to meet reason's needs for knowledge and completeness.

Ironically, only the antinomies—which seem most decisively to bring reason into conflict with itself—can supply a way to heal this rift, at least after a fashion. The "I think," asserted as independent of the series of conditions which it surveys and judges in accord with other laws of varying kinds and scopes, becomes transformed into a thought that may be expressed as "I give myself and so bind myself to a law, the moral law." With this free intelligible action, God and immortality are rerouted from a place—theoretical reason—where they can only provoke discord and confusion to a place where they can bring at least a certain measure of concord and clarity.

This measure can be indicated in the following way. Any connection between activities performed from the moral law and my happiness as a natural being is an uncertain one. The idea of God represents the eventual synthesis of such freedom-determined actions and natural necessity, i.e., of virtue and happiness, projected into an indefinite but imaginable future. Similarly, the idea of immortality represents the eventual synthesis of my rational nature with its complete victory over pathological desire. This victory is also projected into an indefinite but in principle imaginable future. By contrast with the syntheses of theoretical reason that thwart the formation of images in the Dialectic of Pure Reason, the syntheses of practical reason further the fashioning of images, in this case pure images of a possible future for me.

Further, these practical images are *vicarious* images, images that are *lived through* by a self-determining subject. Life, Kant says in an early footnote, is "the faculty of a being by which it acts according to the laws of the faculty of desire" (V, 9n). But ours is a bifurcated faculty of desire, one stem of which behaves according to the law of natural causality (pathological desire), and the other of which can behave in accord with the moral law. Human life cannot, then, see itself whole except in terms of the synthesis of the two stems. In other words, human life cannot form an image of its nature except as a projected possibility of the togetherness of happiness and virtue, and this virtue is unimaginable except as the analogue of an infinitely progressing albeit always morally imperfect soul.

On the surface, then, the objective reality of the ideas of God and immortality consists of their attachment to the necessary and, in that sense, objective presupposition of freedom. In the depths, however, this reality makes itself manifest in the outcome of the synthesis of imagination which effects this attachment. The object created by productive imagination by means of its syntheses is the pure image of a good human life. Both the moral struggle itself and the necessary end toward which this struggle aims are captured in the image-play of freedom and the two ideas that would otherwise remain consigned to eternal dysfunction.[38]

PART 1

Analytic of Pure Practical Reason

ὁδὸς ἄνω κ'ʹτω μία καὶ ὡυτή

[The path up and down is the same.]
—Heraclitus

Principles of Pure Practical Reason

Imagination and Moral "Derivation"

The use of pure reason, if it is shown that there is such a reason [i.e., a use that can determine the will] is constituted such that it is alone immanent; the empirically contingent use of reason, which presumed to be sovereign, is, on the contrary, transcendent, expressing itself in demands and precepts that go far beyond its own sphere. This is precisely the opposite situation from that of pure reason in its speculative use. (V, 16)

In his brief but crucial introduction, Kant goes on to say that his treatment in the Doctrine of Elements will reflect this reversal. It will proceed from principles, to concepts, and only then to sensations, because the concern here is reason's relation to the will and not to objects. Objects must have a sensible component. This sensible component was treated at the outset of the *Critique of Pure Reason* in the Transcendental Aesthetic, but here the concern is the will's relation to an intelligible law.

The first critique, then, presented reason in its *ascent* from intuitions, to imagination, then to apperception as the elements of synthesis and unity. The principles of the pure understanding, in which pure intuition, pure schema, and pure concept converge, represent the apex of this ascent. The "I think" of apperception ultimately means "I think the principles of the pure understanding." But given that the purely formal "I think" requires an act of synthesis in order to make experience possible, productive imagination already dwells at the heart of the "I think."

Why, then, not begin from principles in the critique of speculative reason? Because speculative reason, in seeking the unconditioned, transcends its own apex and in so doing threatens reason's entire enterprise with sham principles that are nevertheless rooted in its nature. The restriction of knowledge to appearances serves as a warning against the *hubris* to which reason is subject in its quest for knowledge of original being and so prevents the *Nemesis* of dialectical illusion.[1] Principles are located *in the middle* of the *Critique of Pure Reason*, imaging reason's holding itself within proper measure.

Again and again, Kant reiterates practical reason's renunciation of any claim to knowledge beyond that measure established by the first critique. The modesty of his claim for the real cognition of practical principles is similarly well-known, and was discussed above.[2] Further, practical principles differ in form from theoretical principles. "Practical principles (*Grundsätze*) are propositions that contain a universal determination of the will which has more practical rules under it" (V, 19). Those rules regarded as valid for a subject's own will are subjective and are called maxims. Those rules that are valid for the will of all rational beings are called laws.

Practical laws always include an "ought," because the subject may always choose not to follow the rule in question. Kant attributes this to our having a faculty of desire such that reason "is not the sole determinant of the will" (V, 20). In terms of imagination and the depth of the Kantian text, this "ought" can be presented otherwise: the *descent* from the law of reason to the faculty of desire is mediated by imagination in a different way than theoretical laws under their principles are mediated to intuition.

Given the spontaneity of synthesis in the principles of theoretical reason and their application by means of the "smart" schemata to our *receptive* intuition, it is impossible to be "transcendentally stupid," although one can surely miscalculate, misread causes, etc. This is because the field of determinable experience is synthesized in advance. By contrast, the principles of practical reason direct themselves not to given appearances, but first to a bifurcated will, and only then to the material served up by sensibility. Just as one can misread appearances presented to the understanding in its theoretical capacity, one can misread moral phenomena. For example, I may keep a promise merely as a means to preserve a reputation I plan to exploit at a later date, while others might read this promise-keeping as occurring entirely from duty (or *vice versa*). Unlike the field of appearances, the moral field is a bifurcated field by its very nature, the contours of which can shift with the shifting influences that constitute the struggle to which we humans are all given over. This makes the phenomena encountered at the bottom of the descent even more difficult to read accurately, although these phenomena are much grosser than, for example, the phenomena of physics that are determinable under the theoretical principles.

Despite both his epistemological modesty and the difficulty of interpreting moral phenomena, Kant says that laws "must sufficiently determine the will as will, even before I ask whether I have the capacity to achieve a desired effect or what should be in order to bring it forth" (V, 20). Even more dramatically, Kant says in the *Foundations* that "the will is nothing other than practical reason" (IV, 412), since only a rational being has the capacity to derive actions "*according to the representation (Vorstellung) of law*" (IV, 412, emphasis in original).

The preparation for the notion of a lawful *imperative*, an "ought" which objectively determines a will that is quite capable of disobedience, is clear. What is not so clear is how any *Vorstellung* serves as a ground of action. In the *Critique of Pure Reason*, Kant presents the divisions of *Vorstellung* as pictured on the following page.

In §16 of the B Deduction, Kant prepares his ultimate account. There, the "I think" is said to be the representation which cannot be derived from any other representation, but which can accompany all of my representations. But from the "I think"—even from the "I think" together with the principles thought through it—not one single object can be derived. Only the most general and minimal determinations flow from them: that any object of experience will have an extensive and intensive magnitude, that it will be determined in some way in terms of time and in relation to the thinking subject. The specific determinations do not even come into play unless the object is not derived but somehow *given*. In this way the synthetic

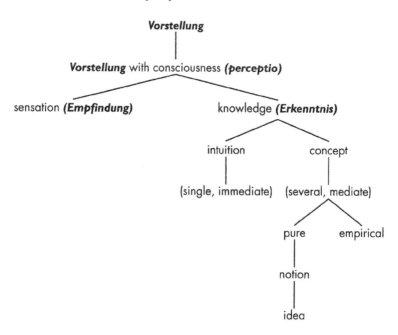

power of imagination holds reason within its proper bounds both in its capacity as producing the field of experience and in its image-making capacity as fashioning objects out of the pure and empirical contents.

But Kant seems to say that *actions themselves* can be derived, and not merely from laws but from the mere representation of a law. How might his four famous examples from the *Foundations,* preserving one's life, truth-telling, showing disinterested kindness toward others, and developing one's talents for the good of humanity, be understood as derivations from a representation of the moral law?

The notion of freedom, the idea of reason which is the *ratio essendi* of the law, is that representation that will serve either as a first premise of which the action is the conclusion, or as a ground of which the action is the consequent (depending upon how "derivation" is understood). It is also clear that there is mediation; a *maxim,* either universalizable or not, serves as the proximate ground of an action. Thus, for example, any individual case of truth-telling is derived from the universalizability of that maxim according to

which one must always tell the truth, which is itself a particulariza-
tion of the moral law which commands that all maxims serve as
principles establishing universal law. Since there is much more conceptual material contained in the maxim than in the law, the fashioning of the maxim is an act of synthesis and therefore the work of
imagination.

But this is hardly the end of imagination's work in the "derivation." In another astonishing sentence, this one from the Preface to
the *Foundations*, Kant exposes a chasm between moral law and action
that transforms the practice of derivation:

> No doubt these [moral] laws require a power of judgment (*Urtheilskraft*)
> sharpened by experience, partly in order to decide in what cases they
> apply and partly to procure for them an access to man's will and an
> impetus to their practice, since humanity is affected by so many inclina-
> tions that, though he is capable of the idea of a pure, practical reason,
> he is not so easily able to make it effective *in concreto* in the conduct of
> his life. (V, 389)

Before proceeding further into more difficult issues, note how decisively Kant declares that the application of the moral laws is *anything but* a matter of straightforward derivation, logical or otherwise. The power of judgment (*Urteilskraft*), the work of imagination
whereby an intuition is supplied under a concept in the theoretical
realm, is also required in the practical realm. It is required not merely
to supply an instance of a concept correctly, but to supply an action
that faithfully instantiates the moral law. How inane to seek extreme
counterexamples in order to undermine the universality of the moral
law! How foolish to think that any example that might seem "intuitively" in conflict with the moral law could serve as a refutation of
it![3] Without the universalizable maxim of truth-telling, not only is
any rational philosophy impossible, but so too is science. This is the
Kantian position. But the step from the maxim to the action is a step
across the intelligible/sensible divide. This is a step that may at times
require a cultivated imagination.[4]

Viewing this situation from the standpoint of the situated human
being, and with the representation of the moral law serving as first
premise or ground, what can be concluded? From "above," there is

the moral law as the pure image of law that serves as the standard for the various moral laws (derivatives of the categorical imperative, such as those which govern the four examples), which are *its* images. From "below," there is the multifarious manifold of inclinations, holding out *their* images. The human being finds herself or himself located in the midst of this interplay of images, situated just as firmly in the middle as in the *Critique of Pure Reason*.

Reason's ascent to the unconditioned led to the *Nemesis* of dialectical illusion, to a thwarted image-play. What is the outcome of reason's descent from the moral law founded on the intelligible notion of freedom to action in the actual human world? As noted above, although these actions can be more easily discernible, their moral content—their *intention*—remains dark, closed off to a significant degree even to the actor.[5] While Kant regards the natural interest of human beings in the discussion of moral matters as a source of optimism, it is the combination of the relatively easy discernibility of actions together with the darkness of their source that animates such discussions.

The outcome of the descent, then, is this: unlike the field of experience upon which objects appear and recede (i.e., show themselves) according to laws, on the moral field not only does nothing whatsoever appear,[6] but the moral field itself recedes. This field can only be brought into being through the free imaginative act of the human subject giving herself or himself laws and by obeying those laws, without there being any other firm evidence of the field's reality. In other words, only by means of such an act can the human being fashion a rational moral realm for herself or himself within which life can be meaningfully carried on. Further, only by means of this free imaginative act whereby the reality of this field is asserted can a system of reason be envisioned at all.

Comments upon §1

Kant's distinctions between practical principles, practical rules that are rules for the will of every rational being, and maxims, which merely express a ground for the action of my own will, have occasioned some interesting discussion. But I think it is far more revealing of Kant's moral philosophy to focus once again upon the *strangeness* of Kant's procedure and example here. It does not seem clear at all that, for example, one who holds the maxim that no offense should go unavenged can at once see that this is not a practical law and, if taken as such, would be inconsistent with itself. The Achillean revenge-seeker seems to be the last person who would pause and reflect upon the logical status of her or his maxim.

But *assuming* that the revenge-seeker is a rational being, he or she *can* so reflect. Kant never says more than this, that the ability of a rational being to determine the will is a necessary assumption that must be asserted. In other words, rational nature is itself a pure image that the bifurcated human being holds before itself as its own (synthetic, i.e., imagination-generated) principle. So the maxim "no offense (*Beleidigung*) is to be tolerated unrevenged" fails the test, because if it were made a rule for all rational beings, it "could not agree with itself (*mit sich selbst nicht zusammen stimmen könne*)" (V, 19). However, the rule that one must never make a deceitful promise passes the test: Kant says that "[i]t is a law because it is a categorical imperative" (V, 21).

But deceitful promises seem clearly not only permissible, but even enjoined under certain circumstances, including the famous case which Kant addresses concerning the would-be murderer asking for the location of his innocent would-be victims. And revenge, at least in its outward manifestation, seems clearly not only permissible, but even enjoined in certain cases, such as the punishment of political opponents after an unjust, brutal, and unsuccessful coup attempt. In his Remark (*Anmerkung*) to the Elucidation (*Erklärung*) in §1, Kant takes no notice of such apparent anomalies. But just as the way up in the first *Critique* led to the difficulties disclosed in the Dialectic of Pure Reason, the way down in the second *Critique* seems to culminate in difficulties which are perhaps even more vexing.

But just as Kant never claims that reason can completely determine the will, he also never claims that reason can give a univocal answer in every single moral quandary in this life. What is clear from the Remark to §1 is this: the "ought" of the categorical imperative, in commanding absolutely, takes no account of desired effects or purposes. That is to say, its calculus is not derived from the world of sense at all, but from that free act of pure imagination which both fashions the moral law (from material supplied by the pure understanding freed from its bond to sense) and installs reason as capable of employing this law as the sufficient ground of action. Moral philosophy can do nothing more, and nothing else can establish moral philosophy.

Comments upon §2, Theorem I

Practical principles that presuppose *objects* (Kant's emphasis) of the faculty of desire are one and all empirical, and so cannot be laws. The conception of such an object in its relation to a subject, Kant says, is called *pleasure* (*Lust*) in the reality of the object. It is clear that such principles fail the test of both objective and subjective universality, because the calculus of pleasure in objects is indeterminate.

Despite the non-universality associated with particular judgments concerning them, pleasure and displeasure (*Unlust*) can clearly be, often are, and perhaps to some degree are always grounds of choice (*Willkür*). Their particular instances are the natural causes and effects that are at play in the realm of freedom. But because of their variability within and among human beings and because of their non-rational nature, the deduction from the moral law results in their exclusion from moral philosophy. Thus, they both belong and do not belong to moral philosophy.

In the language of imagination, they present a very strange kind of image: at once real, i.e., tied to the intensive fulfillment of a projection of pathological desire, and ideal, i.e., toward pleasure and away from displeasure in the most general sense. Whether it is a craving for a particular object (e.g., a gluttonous desire for a certain food), the quest for a more general and non-sensuous object (e.g., honor), or the desire for the stature of a simple moral human being, one has a vague but not entirely indistinct image of that object. One might say that the pure imagination that fashions the categorical imperative for a will smears itself with the stuff of real images so soon as pleasure and displeasure enter.

But continuing Kant's discussion of *life* as consisting of action in accord with the laws of the faculty of desire (*Begehrungsvermögen*), he writes:

> the faculty of desire is the faculty such a being has of causing, through its representations, the reality of the objects of those representations. *Pleasure (Lust)* is the representation of the agreement of object or action with the *subjective* conditions of life, i.e., with the faculty through which the representation causes the reality of its object (or the direction of the energies of a subject to such an action as will produce its object). (V, 9n)

Thus pleasure (and pain) is *always* a factor in human life, and so is always at play in human judgment. Our bifurcated faculty of desire guarantees some degree of smearing.

Of course, this is as far as possible from saying that there are no purely moral judgments. Just as the principles of the pure understanding have objective validity but are without real content apart from the empirical intuitions they determine, the categorical imperative has the objective validity peculiar to moral judgments but has no real content apart from determining the maxims of actions. Just as the ill-fated ascent from intuitions to concepts to the unconditioned is a genuine ascent and one which reason necessarily undergoes in its quest for unity, the descent from principles to maxims to actions is a genuine descent, although it too is fated to shatter against the limits to which it is given over.

Comments upon §3

"Self-love" and "one's own happiness" denote the representation of pleasure extended to a maximum. All material principles belong under their principle. So a certain kind of universality grounds every material principle, a principle that might be expressed as "all human beings move toward pleasure and/or away from displeasure." As

Kant shows in his first Remark under this section, this standpoint of the other stem of the bifurcated faculty of desire determines every orientation toward pleasure, whether an object of the senses or an object of the intellect provokes this determination.

Thus, either all desire is oriented toward pleasure, or there is another, heterogeneous faculty of desire—pure practical reason. Again, "[s]ubordinate to reason as the higher faculty of desire is the pathologically determinable faculty of desire, the latter being really and *specifically* different from the former" (V, 25, emphasis in original). The first Remark, then, characterizes the descent as a descent across a chasm. On the other side of pure practical reason lie pleasure-promising images both of the senses and of the intellect. While the intellectual pleasures have already been said to have their uses in the life of a moral human being, they cannot serve in the least to ground that life.

The second Remark under this section is among the most significant in the history of philosophy. What are we? We are finite, each human being is *a being of needs*. Our happiness? It is not given to us. It is a problem for us. Our morality is not given to us either. The pathway to our rational homecoming is at least partially hidden, perhaps overgrown in other parts. Our freedom, then, is the freedom of a doubly alienated being.

But this freedom, as Kant has maintained from the outset, is bound up with lawfulness, namely the capacity to give ourselves our own law. But, he argues here, no material principles can provide this lawfulness since such principles are rooted in ever-shifting desires and capacities associated with the general desire for happiness. Such desires and capacities can vary even within the same individual. "[The desire for happiness] can therefore yield no [practical[7]] law, because in the desire for happiness it is not the *form* of lawfulness (*Gesetzmäßigkeit*) but only the material which is decisive" (V, 25, emphasis mine).

The well-known logical name Kant gives this form is "categorical imperative." This form, however, issues from a source that lies deeper than mere logic can reach. This form is synthetic. Thus, this form is the product of imagination. We comprehend only its incomprehensibility. Only actions whose maxims accord with this form are moral actions. Even if there were unanimity upon the issue of pleasure and pain both in terms of objects and in terms of means, this unanimity would have no moral force. This distinction between formal and material principles, by virtue of which the former yields laws while the latter cannot, "defines the most important distinction which can be considered in practical investigations" (V, 26).

What, then, is a human being? A being of needs, a being of *lacks:* lacking access to originals with respect to knowledge, lacking the capacity to liberate oneself entirely from the causal chain determined by pathological desire, but able to formulate a law the full obedience to which is always just out of reach. The imagery associated with such a being may seem to be best associated with tragedy, as the earlier mentions of *hubris* and *Nemesis* indicated. Here in the moral realm, the proscription against declaring any of one's own actions to be entirely free of self-love serves as a caution against that *hubris.*

However, and just as surely, the image of the human being as a *comic* figure resonates as well. Socrates gleefully declaring his contempt for those below while swinging from a basket in the heavens in Aristophanes' *Clouds* can be seen as an inverted ridiculous image of Kant's attempt to separate out the truly pure element from the lifeforce to which we are all subject. This is, once again, as far as possible from saying that these distinctions are meaningless, or even that they are not the most important distinctions for a human being to make in leading a good life. It is merely to note that the very attempt to fashion a pathway that is most crucial to human life carries with it the guarantee that every human being will behave ignominiously at some points while traversing it. The way down from form through maxims to actions can thus culminate in such a comic image.

However, the tragic and the comic alike belong to an image play that they hardly exhaust.[8]

Comments upon §4, Theorem III

Kant treated form as the negation of matter in the previous section. Here he asserts that "mere form" is the ground of universal law, and by its means, serves as the ground of all practical laws. The mere form of maxims, "according to which *they are suitable for universal lawgiving,* alone makes them practical laws" (V, 27, emphasis in original).

If the way down as shown in the previous section culminates in possibilities that are tragic or comic, this section holds out a human possibility that escapes both outcomes. Kant calls the universality of the moral law an "identical and therefore self-evident" proposition. He claims that a law as a ground of action that would not hold in all cases, i.e., that would not completely determine the will, would not be a law at all but merely a general guide. Kant's example of an action guided by such a sham law is an act of avarice whereby one retains a deposit placed by someone who has died and of which there is no record. Clearly, Kant says, the maxim according to which one may keep a deposit if there is no proof of its having been made (i.e., "one may retain a deposit illicitly") would annihilate itself if universalized, since no deposits would then be made.

Kant's contempt for morality based upon self-love or happiness is as thorough as it is famous. His examples, however, expose two different aspects of this categorical opposition. The first, discussed above, is that such maxims annihilate themselves. His two other examples show another aspect, namely a more general absurdity inherent in the notion that any maxim based upon individual happiness can serve as a ground of *universal* law: (a) a married couple finds each spouse "harmoniously" wishing the misery of the other, and (b) both the Emperor Charles and his estranged brother Francis I "come to agreement" in that they each covet Milan. There is no inner contradiction in these examples, but they serve to expose an absurdity at their heart.[9]

But in all these cases governed by maxims based upon happiness (or misery and/or enmity, its kindred analogues), and unlike those cases determined by the categorical imperative, the way down from maxim to action is *clear,* at least in principle. The desire for money resulting in the receipt of money, the desire for revenge resulting in its attempted promulgation, and the desire for power resulting in its exercise (or loss) one and all follow as if they were immediate inferences from an Aristotelian universal judgment. Unlike moral actions, which have their source in principles concealed from external and even (to a degree) internal view, actions done from the maxim of happiness are out in the open.

This reversal of the order of ascent/descent in the realm of the practical yields this paradox: while maxims based upon the desire for happiness result in obvious but often blatantly absurd results (their actions can be directly immoral, or two such motivated actions can contradict one another, etc.), it is "astonishing" according to Kant that happiness has been so widely extolled as the ground of morality when it is so clear that this desire has no brake upon it. Accordingly, no universal laws can be fashioned from it. In the language of imagination, this unguided desire draws the human being into a play of images but without any awareness of his or her, or its, finitude. In other words, under the sway of maxims of happiness, the human being mistakes these securely derived images for unproblematic reality and is entirely unaware of his or her true human nature.

Comments upon §5, Task I and upon §6, Problem II

The complete separation in deed of the two fundamental stems of the faculty of desire is impossible, as has been demonstrated. However, both tasks here call for this "impossible" separation. The first task demands that the character of a will determined solely by the legislative form discussed in the previous sections completely sets aside that stem determined by happiness. Such a will is found to be "distinct from all determining grounds of events in nature according to the law of causality" (V, 28). Therefore, the will is free in the transcendental sense, i.e., related entirely to the *a priori* and therefore independent of all experience. The second task locates the "legislative form [and not the material of the law], insofar as it is contained in the maxim" as the only thing that can serve as the determining ground of a free will.

The accomplishment of these two tasks is possible in word (in speech, in reflection), although perhaps never entirely in deed. The Kantian act is most fundamentally an act of *self-reflection,* and it stands in the company not only of the philosophers with whom he is in dialogue and at whom he is "astonished" that they could miss the obvious insufficiency of happiness as ground of moral action. It also recalls the Delphic oracle that has set the task for philosophers. In the Kantian re-enactment of the oracle, moral self-knowledge is ongoing and never completed, requiring ever-sustained self-examination.[10]

In a revealing parenthetical comment, Kant says that we become *immediately* conscious of the moral law that presents itself *as soon as we project maxims of the will to ourselves* (V, 29–30).[11] Why is this consciousness called "immediate?" Because a maxim by its nature possesses a legislative form, and this form constitutes the moral law. Projecting a maxim includes projecting the form of a maxim. Whether one is "conscious of this consciousness" is another matter, just as it is in the first critique: transcendental apperception is always present whether it is conceived as such or not.

This consciousness is possible "insofar as we pay attention (*Acht haben*) to the necessity that reason prescribes, and to the separation from all empirical conditions"[12] (V, 30). The concept of a pure will arises when this act of attention is performed in the practical realm, while the consciousness of a pure understanding occurs in the theoretical realm. Thus "know yourself" here means "attend to the necessity prescribed by reason." Pure will and pure understanding, disclosed by means of this attention, at once provide self-knowledge together with its limits. We know ourselves only as we appear to ourselves, and the ultimate intentions of our actions are closed off from us as well.

But this act of attention also discloses the fields of real knowledge and of dignified action for a human being. Recalling the role of freedom as keystone of theoretical reason as well, the search for real knowledge itself belongs to the field of dignified action. Both tasks set by Kant are performed by an ongoing act of attention and by the associated ongoing reflection upon one's pursuits.

Again, this act of reflection, this attention to the *necessity* that reason prescribes, does not yield either theoretical or practical knowledge. Rather, it yields the condition for the possibility for such knowledge. The necessity that reason prescribes is neither merely logical nor merely causal. The act of attention to reason's necessity in its theoretical employment yields a *transcendental* logic, i.e., a logic of conditions to which an object must conform in order to be an object for us. Its analogue in the practical realm is a causality in which the pure form of a law can serve as a ground of universalizable maxims, i.e., a logic of imperatives for a free being, or a standard to which all maxims must conform in order to be moral maxims.

These twin necessities are not "things in themselves" or "things" at all. They are *pure images* through which knowledge and moral action become possible. As such, they are *vicarious* images as well, images through which a rational life is lived by a human being. If there is no act of attention, there can be no consciousness of these necessities. And if there is no further act of reflection upon these necessities such as the one I have just performed, their genuine nature remains concealed and distorted. Until and unless the Kantian philosophy is grasped fundamentally in terms of its ongoing awareness and disclosure of its own limits, an awareness that has shaped the philosophical enterprise since Socrates challenged his fellow Athenians, the main issues of his moral philosophy will continue to be misrepresented.

Kant's example of a man who, under prospect of death, is enjoined to testify to his sovereign against an honorable man the ruler wished to destroy under some false pretext, gives excellent access to one central issue. While the person under pressure may decide either way, it is clear that there *are* two ways, two grounds of choice from which he *can* decide, and thus he is free even in the face of death. The kinship to the *logoi* of Socrates in the *Apology,* that a good man considers only what is right and does not consider death or any other concern when deciding to act,[13] is unmistakable.

Comments upon §7

This section is introduced by the categorical imperative itself: "So act that the maxim of your will could always hold (*gelten könne*) at the same time as a principle establishing universal law" (V, 30). Much of the material in the first part of this section, concerning the facticity of the moral law together with its strangeness, has already been discussed above. The corollary provides something even stranger: the notion of a perfect will, which Kant calls a *holy* will. No maxims can conflict with the moral law in such a will. Thus it makes no sense to speak of the obligations attending to a holy will. Only a finite but rational will, like ours, has obligations.

Kant's conception of an "infinite being as the highest intelligence" (V, 32) seems to mirror the being spoken of in Section §8, Part IV of the Transcendental Aesthetic of the *Critique of Pure Reason*, in which the infinite being has an intuitive intelligence that creates the objects in the very act of knowing them. But in the former *Critique*, Kant is careful to say that this notion is presented for purposes of illustration only, namely the illustration of our own finite intellect as requiring "thought, which always involves limitations" (B71). There is no exhortation there that we ought to strive to imitate such a being. Here, however, the holy will is called a "necessary *Urbilde*" (V, 32), usually translated as archetype or model, but literally connotes an *originary* or *primal image.*

Clearly, the holy will is no object of experience. Nor, strictly speaking, is it a thought, since it corresponds to none of the ideas of pure reason. Rather, the holy will is the pure product of creative imagination, fashioning an image for itself out of its own materials. It is the work of a finite being fashioning a moral image of infinitude that honors both the freedom and the limits to which *humanity* is given over.[14] By contrast, the theological treatment in which God is treated metaphysically as the *ens realissimum*, exposed in the first critique's Ideal of Pure Reason, leads to dialectical illusion with its attendant confusions.

The holy will enjoins no particular action. Rather, as "a practical idea" (V, 32), a certain posture toward the holy will is regarded as morally *necessary;* all rational beings must hold the moral law "constantly and rightly before their eyes" in order to assure constant progress in the formation of practical reason's maxims and the unwavering attitude (*Unwandelbarkeit*) of the finite rational being in making continuous progress toward the *Urbild.* "Constant" means steady in holding up the moral law according to its form as the ground of action. "Right" means "for the sake of the law itself" or "from duty itself," and not for any consequences beyond this.

Kant concludes §7 by reminding that virtue is "a naturally acquired[15] faculty that can never be perfect (*vollendet*), because assurance in such cases can never be an apodictic certainty, and as persuasion (*Überredung*) it is very dangerous" (V, 33). Once again, the moral issue for Kant is neither the action nor its consequence, but the quality of the will. One of the tasks of §7 is to locate the good will in terms of its *Urbild*, the holy will. The holy will, as has been seen, is a will that is entirely one with itself; its maxims are one and all in accord with the moral law. Thus, the good will is the will that always focuses itself on the holy will, on this "one." In so doing, the human being is not focusing on anything distant or out of this world, but rather is focusing upon the appropriate unity which he or she seeks out of our bifurcated, doubly alienated nature.

Comments upon §8, Theorem IV

Autonomy of the will is called both the positive sense of freedom and the principle of all moral laws. The first characterization is self-evident from the literal meaning of the word. The second requires some exegesis concerning how the quality of a will can be a principle (*Prinzip*). This will be supplied below. *Heteronomy* is not nearly so straightforward. The literal meaning of "heteronomy," rule by another, is also clear. But Kant stresses that heteronomy entails no obligations and, further, that it is opposed to duty and to the moral law.

The initial discussion focuses upon the *formal* nature of the reciprocity between the autonomy of the will and the moral law. Not only is "the mere form of giving universal law" the ground of all moral maxims, but the autonomy of pure practical reason (the will) is "the *formal* condition of *all* maxims" (V, 33, emphasis mine). This is different in its language but no different in substance than the discussion of the holy will in the previous section. In this section, Kant speaks the language of logic and not of image-making; the task for a human being is to choose maxims that bring its "capable-of-any-maxim-forming" will into conformity with the mere form of giving universal law. The first Remark, however, addresses a concern that is far from merely logical. A human being has a bifurcated faculty of desire, and since the stem associated with self-love or happiness can never be entirely silenced, something must be done to incorporate it into the unity of the moral law. Moreover, there can be no wish to silence it, since it is a necessary condition for *life,* and the preservation of life is one of the moral duties, perhaps the first one of all.[16] But principles based upon my own happiness are one and all heteronomous, and so cannot serve as the ground of any moral principles.

Clearly, any maxim that is grounded by happiness in any sense (including universal assent) is heteronomous and so excluded from morality. Only "the formal conditions of the possibility of a law in general" or "the mere form of a law" is a suitable ground for moral maxims. But material *may be added to the will,* not presupposed (*zum Willen hinzufügen, aber sie nicht voraussetzen*) (V, 34, emphasis in the translation mine), Kant says, so long as it is limited by the mere form of a law, and thus so long as the material makes the maxim universalizable. Therefore and for example, by making the furtherance of the happiness of others my maxim, for example, I have satisfied the condition.

This maxim is a synthetic judgment, and is therefore the work of imagination. But it seems to involve another aspect of imagination as well, namely an ability to fashion a happiness that is entirely intelligible in nature out of the material given through one's own pathological desire for happiness. Intelligible happiness—happiness as the pure material of a pure maxim—this creative transformation of the pathological into the spontaneous is one of imagination's most remarkable deeds.

In the "Canon of Pure Reason" in the Doctrine of Method of the *Critique of Pure Reason,* Kant refers to the sensible world in which real human beings (in the theoretical sense) dwell as a "*corpus mysticum*" from the standpoint of the moral world "so far as the free will of each being is, under moral laws, in complete systematic unity with itself and with the freedom of every other" (A808, B837). This idea, called by the more modest name of a "realm of ends (or purposes)

(*Zwecke*)" (IV, 433–34) in the *Foundations,* echoes the purely intelligible nature of humanity sounded in the former. But this peculiar reciprocal imaging of sensible and intelligible signals nothing other than our embodiment, with its attendant needfulness and finitude, that makes such an imaginative transformation both possible and necessary, and for the sake of which this transformation takes place.

Thus, the descent from principle through maxim to action pictured in this Remark gives a closer view of the aforementioned smearing of pure imagination and the images to which we are given over as a result of our embodied nature. According to the measure of our pathological desire, these images are the real correlates of our desire for pleasure and for avoidance of pain. Again, according to this measure alone only natural causality is at work; the autonomy of the will has no force. But allow the freedom of the will to enter, and imagination transforms the aggregate of pathologically determined human beings into a union of moral beings who are "mysteriously embodied" and whose desires can be inconveniences and hindrances to the true nature of each human being and to the human community as a whole.

In this light, those once powerful pathological causes are transformed from dangerous obstacles to a good life into playful opponents in a game for which we humans are quite well equipped, and to which we might return with good hope even after a series of defeats. This transformation (among others) drives the interpretation here in this regard, namely to redirect attention from the causal concerns in the text to imagination and the play of images that constitutes their depth. In the same way, the moral struggle that was spoken of earlier can be viewed in this more playful light and so regarded without an excessive seriousness.[17]

The Second Remark in this section stresses (a) the opposition (*Widerspiel*) to morality and the ruin morality would suffer if maxims of happiness were allowed to determine the will and (b) the obviousness of this insight to even the commonest understanding. Leibnizian clarity and obscurity were set aside as ways to distinguish concepts in theoretical philosophy. Instead, the place of origin of a concept proved decisive there. Here in practical philosophy, where the sensible/intelligible distinction plays a far greater role, so too does clarity. Under the autonomy of choice (*Willkür*), what duty requires is "entirely easy to see and without deliberation (*Bedenken*)." It "presents itself from itself to everyone (*bietet sich jedermann von selbst dar*)" (V, 36). By contrast, what heteronomy requires is veiled in impenetrable obscurity and requires knowledge of the world in order to select suitable means toward the security of one's particular happiness.[18] In a stunning leap, Kant moves from the ease and clarity of moral conception to the power of satisfying what this conception commands. "It is at all times in everyone's power to satisfy the commands of the categorical command of morality; this is but seldom possible with the empirically conditioned precept of happiness, and it is far from being possible, even in respect to a single purpose, for everyone. . . . Whatever [someone] wills to do in this relation [of obedience/non-obedience to the moral law], he can also do" (V, 36–37).

This passage is reminiscent of the footnote from the *Foundations* cited above, in which the twofold synthesis connects (a) the will itself with its moral principle opposed to the dictates of inclination and (b) the moral principle with the action. This addition of the second fold is precisely what makes *autonomy* the positive sense of freedom. Human beings can discern moral maxims that conform to the categorical imperative and *can* act in accord with those maxims.

In no way does any of this contradict or even challenge either the darkness surrounding the moral law, surrounding all moral motives, or surrounding the actions putatively issuing from them. This "*can*" belongs to the assertoric nature of freedom and has no other epistemic meaning. In the Canon of Pure Reason, Kant employs and emphasizes a subjunctive when discussing the parallel between speculative and practical possibility of experience:

> Pure reason, then, contains, not indeed in its speculative employment, but in that practical employment which is also moral, principles of the possibility of *experience*, namely of such *actions* as, in accordance with the moral precepts, *might* be met with in the *history* of mankind (*in der Geschichte des Menschen anzutreffen sein könnten*. (A807, B835, emphasis on "actions" mine; other emphases in original)

Knowledge from principles, as defined in the *Critique of Pure Reason*, refers to the apprehension of the particular in a universal through concepts (A300, B357). Theoretical reason applies its threefold principle of systematic unity directly to the understanding by means of the schemata-analoga of imagination, and only then indirectly to experience. Practical knowledge from the principle of autonomy follows a similarly indirect and "downward" course, first to maxims of the categorical imperative (whose content exceeds the imperative although it is limited by it) to actions that *may* be read as issuing from moral maxims.

Kant's examples are best understood not as illustrations of a universal law, but as provocative images designed to aid in the conception of the law that is already clearly presupposed in any fashioning of examples.[19] The image of a man losing at play and blaming himself for imprudence and another of a man (perhaps the same man) winning at play but holding himself in contempt for cheating solicits two different responses in terms of two different measures. It is a *modus tollens* proof:[20] if there were not two measures, then there would not be these two different responses. Thus it may be "inadvisable" (but not a command) to gamble, although given a high skill level and poor players one might decide differently according to a measure determined by prudence. But it is always "evil" to cheat, since honesty is commanded.

The clarity of the pure image of the moral law enables everyone, at least in principle, to act in accord with moral maxims derived from it. The issue of just punishment raised in this context likewise gives rise to a *modus tollens*, although in a different direction: only if a pre-established law is transgressed does the notion of deserved punishment make any sense. In both the example of the gambler and that of the criminal, the actor has brought the difficulty upon himself. With respect to specifically moral "difficulty," there is no escaping the principle of autonomy if human actions are to have any meaning *qua* human, i.e., *qua* rational, at all.

The classification of the "material" principles follows directly from Theorem 4. It is plain that Kant excludes certain aspects of the intelligible from form, namely its determination of (both theoretical and practical) experience through concepts alone. Just as plainly, he includes imagination; the pure form of a law is synthetic, spontaneously produced, and capable of crossing the intelligible/sensible divide. The right of this crossing to occur will form the subject matter of the transcendental deduction in the *Critique of Practical Reason*.

I. OF THE DEDUCTION OF THE PRINCIPLES OF PURE PRACTICAL REASON

Concerning this deduction, Kant says, "[O]ne cannot hope to have it come forth as well as it did (*nicht so gut*) with the principles of pure theoretical reason" (V, 46). This is not only because the deduction in the theoretical critique has the advantage of recourse to pure intuition, but also because the deduction in the practical critique appeals to an "inscrutable faculty" (*eines unerforschliches Vermögens*) (V, 47), namely the faculty of freedom. The parallel to the place of the deductions within their respective critiques also seems strained: Where in the theoretical critique the deduction of the twelve categories and the determination of their schemata are presented as gathered in principles that determine all appearances, in the practical critique the moral law is the "premise" from which the faculty of freedom is "deduced." From the latter, the intelligible world, in which reason becomes "in the field of experience, an efficient cause through ideas"[21] (V, 48), is inferred. In the latter deduction, then, only the category of causality among the twelve comes into play. Further, the moral principle itself serves as the sole source of the realm in which it is to function.

At its outset, Kant bundles three elements that constitute this realm: (1) the fact of "autonomy, in the principle of morality by which reason determines the will to action" (V, 42), (2) the inextricable bond of this fact to the "consciousness of freedom" with which it is "equivalent (*einerlei*)" (V, 42), and (3) regarding the latter consciousness "certain dynamic laws that determine its causality in the world of sense" (V, 42). Only by analogy to the natural law of causality, itself a synthetic *a priori* principle, can this synthetically unified realm be thought to have any efficacy.

Principles of Pure Practical Reason

But "the field of experience," also called *nature*, is also the realm in which theoretical reason functions. In the first critique, nature is defined as "the connection of appearances as regards their existence according to necessary rules, that is, according to laws" (A216, B263). Nature in the second critique, supersensuous nature, is presented as a twofold. The first "fold" is called *natura archetypa* and is the correlate of reason itself. The second is called *natura ectypa*, which is the correlate of *natura archetypa* and which determines the will by means of intelligible causality.[22] To understand this deduction, it is crucial to note that at no juncture does Kant ever declare that there really is a connection between supersensuous and sensuous nature. The capability of the human being to execute actions in the field of experience in accord with moral maxims is not an issue at all. "*The will's power* (**Vermögen**) *in execution may be what it may*" (V, 45–46, emphasis mine on entire passage, emphasis on *Vermögen* in original).

Gathering up the elements issuing from this deduction, the following list gives the outcome: (1) a will which is indifferent to its ability to secure what it wills; (2) three images of nature which need not interact, and in which not one single object is determined; and (3) an inscrutable faculty that serves as the source of the entire practical edifice, derived from a law whose comprehensibility is withheld from us. Darkness thus haunts pure practical reason, just as it haunts its theoretical counterpart. However, one can surely, through great labors, discover rules and laws according to which reason operates and can even discern their nature, their scope, and their limits. But the most painstaking exposition cannot expunge the darkness of the origin and the darkness surrounding the necessary and even shining light that such a critical exposition can bring.

In theoretical reason, the schemata of pure productive imagination serve to establish the connection between the categories and pure intuition. But empirical inspection is required in order to learn anything particular about nature. There are no such schemata of pure practical reason, and hence no mediation between concept (law) and object in general. What, then, does pure practical reason provide in the way of determining or producing its objects? It provides this idea of a moral law that, but for our physical shortcomings, would bring forth the highest good and would "impart to the sensuous world the *form* of a whole of rational beings" (V, 43, emphasis mine). This idea "lies as a drawing of a model (*als Vorzeichnung zum Muster liege*)," accessible by means of "the most common attention to oneself" (V, 43). The contrast to the Schematism, which Kant calls "an art concealed in the depths of the human soul" (A142, B181), could not be stated more starkly. For the idea of the moral law, one need only attend directly to oneself to discover this remarkable drawing of its model.

Within the deduction, Kant employs two of his most frequently used moral examples, truth-telling and life-affirmation. These examples can be regarded anew in light of the results of the aforementioned self-attention. Our drawing-model of ourselves as free rational beings capable of determining our own actions constrains the images that can be drawn in accord with it. In other words, the detailed contours of lying[23] and of suicide cannot be filled in at all given the constraints imposed by this model. Untruthfulness in bearing witness cannot serve as a law of (practical) nature first and foremost because such lying cannot be inscribed into the drawing of law-abiding rational nature. Nor can suicide be inscribed into such a nature, for which the furtherance of life belongs to its law. In such inscriptions, the model could not be discerned at all.

Such "conclusions" concerning particular matters, far from exceeding the scope of the formal character Kant ascribes to the idea of the moral law in its influence upon sensation, hold us human beings within the limits to which we are given over. In this sense, they may be interpreted as markers, warnings against transgressing the appropriately human limits (*hubris*). Kant's own image-language leads to their impossibility of construction by productive imagination in accord with the idea of ourselves as rational beings as disclosed through the moral law. Given that there are no laws of (practical) nature other than the ones freely prescribed to it, reason can walk properly into the darkness only by means of a path suitable to its own nature and needs. This pathway requires that productive imagination be able to provide an image for the human being that can appropriately orient life.

Of course witnesses can and often do give willfully false testimony in nature as appearance. Suicides also occur. Their occurrences and images in life, as in literature and the arts, are many and various. Given the heterogeneous determination of the will—given, that is, our pathological nature as determining ground of the will as well— imagination has little difficulty attending to the causal chain that issues from such pathological impulses as fear, greed, desire for revenge, desire for escape from pain, and the like. Only in the ideal realm of pure, univocally determined nature, does productive imagination find itself constrained, able to form no such acceptable moral image. In terms of logic, such self-repellent notions (truth-telling/ lying, life-affirmation/suicide) clearly cannot determine the will at all, for as contradictions they cannot even be thought. Hence, imagination can generate no image at all from such a disfigured non-model. Willfully false testimony can and often does emerge, but only when reason's other, pathological desire, determines the will such that taking and breaking an oath can appear to issue from one source, when in fact it issues from two.

Obviously, Kant says, no one "in such a nature can (*können*) *willfully* (*willkürlich*, emphasis in original) end his life," for according to a maxim that permits this there would be "no abiding natural order" (V, 44). And, he says, the same is the case in other matters. Here, "in such a nature" clearly means *intelligible* nature, especially if one reads the *können* as a modal present rather than as a subjunctive. An abiding intelligible order implies a will in service to life.

Kant expressed this also in terms more closely associated with the critique of theoretical reason. The form given by the idea of the moral law to the world of sense also entails the reorientation from the transcendent use of reason to its immanent use. Once again, this is called reason's transformation into "an *efficient* cause in the field of experience through ideas themselves" (V, 48, emphasis mine). As shown above, the immanent use of reason requires a limiting of image-making within the drawing-model inscribed *by* our rational nature *of* our rational nature. But the field of experience is an *open* field.[24]

The pure concepts of the understanding with their schemata have no images whatsoever. The appearances themselves—or, in a practical sense, the desires—stand in for the "missing" images. Now the schema of (efficient) causality is "the real upon which, whenever posited, something else always follows" (A144, B183). But the moral law has no direct connection to appearances in time, not even the indirect connection of the appearances to the categories. The moral law, so to speak, *inserts itself into* the causal order of appearances, "alongside" the category in a manner that is and must always remain epistemologically problematic. In so doing, however—in so entering the open image-play of the field of experience in order to attempt to bring it into harmony with itself—it must give itself up in essential ways to this open field. It must itself become part of the play of images—as if it were ever truly anything else.

II. OF THE RIGHT (*BEFÜGNIS*) OF PURE REASON TO AN EXTENSION IN ITS PRACTICAL USE WHICH IS NOT POSSIBLE TO IT IN ITS SPECULATIVE USE

Use (*Gebrauch*)—what does this word mean in the context of pure reason? In the *Critique of Pure Reason,* where the nature and limits of reason as faculty of knowledge are at issue, Kant distinguishes between an immanent and a transcendent use of rational faculties and concepts, restricting the legitimacy of such use to the former. Here in the *Critique of Practical Reason,* where the characteristics of human action in terms of the conflict between what ought to determine it (moral law) and what determines it in terms of the principle of causality on the level of sense are at issue, Kant distinguishes between a theoretical and a practical use.

He famously claims that although the extension of the practical use involves no extension of our knowledge, it nevertheless "widens (*erweitert*) our knowledge beyond the boundaries of sense" (V, 50). How can these two apparently contradictory claims be reconciled?

Much in the manner of the third antinomy, Kant focuses upon the twofold directedness of the concept of causality. For these purposes, an exploration of how this twofold directedness plays itself out in terms of productive imagination is required.

In the previous section, the schema of the concept of causality was exhibited in its role of bringing the appearances under the category. By restricting the category of causality to its immanent use,[25] the concept of causality itself constituted the field of appearances as a play of images whose order could be read off in a certain way. To employ one of Kant's own more well-known examples from the *Prolegomena*, the causal connection between the sun's shine and the stone's warmth can be discerned out of the indefinite and ever-ongoing swirl of sensation. In this example and in others like it, the result is (1) a pure concept (causality), (2) a pure schema that applies this concept to pure intuition, and by its means (3) the actual appearances, all of which constitute a lawful image-play—or, in more prosaic Kantian terms, knowledge.

How does it stand with the practical use of the concept of causality? Consider the *will* with its causality, i.e., man as the subject of a pure will as belonging to an intelligible world. Kant says: "in this relation man is *unknown* to us" (V, 50, emphasis mine). While we can *think* of ourselves as the subject of an efficiently causal will determined by the moral law alone, this is a mere thought and, as Kant also says in the Preface to the Second Edition of the *Critique of Pure Reason*, we can think anything we please just so long as we do not contradict ourselves, but to know something requires connection to an actual object or proof of its possibility through reason (Bxxvin). In this same footnote, Kant allows for there being another kind of real possibility, which "may lie in those [sources] that are practical." Between theoretical and practical sources, however, lies an unbridgeable gulf: "there always remains an infinite unfilled chasm (*Kluft*) between that limit [in which the sensuously conditioned finds its foundation in the unconditioned, if that were possible] and what we know" (V, 55).

Thus *what we think* when we think of a pure will is the sole practical source of the real possibility of practical concepts. Kant presents these thoughts in this section as if they were a series of logical inferences or even definitions:

> But besides the relationship that the understanding has to objects in theoretical knowledge, there is also the relationship in which it stands to the faculty of desire, which is therefore called the will, or the pure will so far as the pure understanding (which is in such a case called reason) is practical through the mere conception of a law. The objective reality of a pure will or of a pure practical reason (they being the same) is given in the moral law *a priori,* as it were by a fact. (V, 55)

> In the concept of a will, however, the concept of causality is already contained; thus in that of a pure will there is the concept of causality with freedom, i.e., of a causality not determinable according to natural laws. . . . Nevertheless, it completely justifies its objective reality. (V, 55)

But if the reciprocal relationship between these moral concepts—will, pure will, pure practical reason, causality, moral law, and the rest of the noumenal firmament—are merely definitional or logical (in the narrow sense), then they fail to establish any connection at all with the sensible world into which they must enter. What is required for the connection of these concepts to one another, and then to the sensible world into which they ought to enter? Clearly synthesis, the work of imagination, is required. But what can imaginative synthesis on the noumenal plane be? And how is this noumenal synthesis conjoined with the world of sense?

Both questions have the same answer. The noumenal synthesis produces (1) intentions (*Gesinnungen*), which should be thought as the willing of the moral law by the pure will, or (2) maxims, which should be thought as those universalizable principles willed in accord with the moral law. In both cases, the causality of the will is presupposed. By means of such causality, the pure will connects with its particular free act of willing. Kant never mentions *actions in the realm of sensation* as indicating or exhibiting real possibility in the practical sphere! This exhibition of "practical reality" is spoken of as "a real application exhibited *in concreto* in intentions and maxims" (V, 56). The intentions and maxims are generated by a synthesis of imagination, a synthesis which assumes that most anomalous of concepts, an atemporal causality. This concept is asserted with the right bestowed by the third antinomy, but its reality and necessity have a practical sense alone.

Thus, the right of the extension of pure reason in its practical use is first, foremost, and always a right of *imagination* to perform syntheses freed from the sensible condition to which theoretical reason is bound. The form of lawfulness in general, that is to say the form of the *synthetic* lawfulness by means of which any experience is possible, is extended only by virtue of this extension of imagination. In other words, this lawful leap of imagination occurs across the chasm separating the spontaneous realm, by virtue of which we can *think* objects, from the receptive realm, by virtue of which we can *intuit* them.

What about this leap, when the "object" in question is ourselves? In the *Critique of Pure Reason*, the Paralogisms clearly establish the non-identity between the "I" that thinks through the categories and the "I" that is thought through the categories. The former is the spontaneous "I" of transcendental apperception, which must accompany all of my representations. The latter is the receptive, phenomenal "I," available only by means of (inner) intuition. But the extension of the concept of causality enables me to think of myself as a noumenon with causal powers reflected in my free adherence to the moral law, although self-knowledge as noumenon is radically closed off to me. Yet this self-ignorant "I," by virtue of its freedom, generates the entire system of reason, including that theoretical reason by means of which these fissures within myself are discovered and ordered so far as they can be!

To conclude this first chapter, then, what can be said about this apparently manifold "I"? The "I think" of theoretical reason says, "I perform a synthesis of imagination by means of the categories which makes experience possible at all." The "I think" of practical reason says, "I perform a synthesis of imagination whereby my intentions and maxims are freely crafted in conformity with the moral law."[26] There appears to be a closing of the gap, a meeting of the two realms, in the concept of causality. Theoretically, I am determined by pathological desire; practically, as noumenon, I can determine myself by moral intentions and maxims. We can never know whether such a meeting is possible. This radical ignorance is the only justification for our extending pure reason in its practical use beyond that possible to it in its theoretical use. This smeared causality, the only hope of real contact, is made possible only by pure productive imagination.

The Concept of an Object of Pure Practical Reason

Imagination, Good and Evil, and the Typic

The central move in the section entitled "The Concept of an Object of Practical Reason" requires close attention. The concepts of good and evil are not given but *constructed*. Guided by the moral law, imagination constructs them. The fault of all previous moral philosophy, both ancient and modern, both rationalist and empiricist, is that the concept of the good was presupposed as the basis and end of morality.[1] The necessary consequence of this presupposition is a heteronomous basis of moral action, such that the good as end is separated from its means.

This is the case whether that means is conceived as pleasure or happiness, or as perfection, or as moral feeling, or as the will of God. The good is regarded as a material end existing outside these means, whether these means are related to the feeling of pleasure and/or general well-being in accord with our natural (animal) desire for happiness, or whether these means are conceived in intelligible terms as objects of a completed reason. Therefore, the relation between means and end always involves an element of contingency, since a good so conceived would be unfit to serve as a basis for "a universally commanding moral law" (V, 65). In other words, all previous moral philosophers proceeded in precisely the opposite way demanded by the subject matter. In the language of the *Foundations,* all moral judgments would be made hypothetically, a condition that conflicts with their very nature.

The only way to preserve moral philosophy from this self-destructive fate, i.e., from this *Nemesis* of inner self-conflict, is to derive the concept of goodness from the nature of reason itself, from reason's own autonomy. But this means that the good is the product of that prior synthesis of imagination whereby the moral law connects with the pure will, and whereby this connection is willed into intentions and maxims. In other words, the good is another pure image in accord with which a human being can orient herself or himself, just as the evil is a pure image that provides a different way of orientation (more on which below). To say this still more strongly, if there is no prior productive synthesis of imagination, then there is no good and no evil.

Good and evil are products of imagination's synthesizing guided by the "pure form of lawfulness in general." In this regard, Kant even says that "laws as such [are] all equivalent (*einerlei*)" (V, 70). That is to say, when imagination carries on its synthesis freed from the sensible condition but guided by the form of law, the image produced from the side of the subject is the moral law as expression of the fact of freedom, and from the side of the object this image is the good as its *immediate* correlate.

In the concept of the good as object of pure practical reason, "the method of the *highest* moral investigation" (V, 64, emphasis mine) and the *depth* of the Kantian discourse in the blind, unconscious but always present power of imagination are conjoined in one act. As noted earlier, the form of a law in general, is not, strictly speaking, a law. Rather, it stands as that equivalent to which all laws must conform in order to qualify as laws. Its counterpart, evil, arises from imagination's synthesizing contrary to that form. There is no middle ground, no stance of indifference.[2] The generated maxim either images the moral law, and so the object immediately generated along with it is good, or it does not, in which case the object so generated is evil.

Of the Typic of Pure Practical Reason

This vital and challenging section seems, however, to exclude both the process of schematization and the imagination itself from the application of the moral law to objects of nature. After speaking of "the schema (if this word is suitable here) of a law itself" (V, 68), and after delineating this process in its capacity to relate pure concepts of the understanding to objects of nature by means of the connection to pure intuition, Kant writes:

> But to the law of freedom (which is a causality not sensuously conditioned), and consequently to the concept of the absolutely good, no intuition and hence no schema can be supplied for the purpose of applying it *in concreto*. Thus the moral law has no other cognitive faculty to mediate its application to objects of nature than the understanding (not the imagination); and the understanding can supply *to an idea of reason* not a schema of sensibility but a law. (V, 69, emphasis on "to an idea of reason" mine)

This "law" is the one Kant calls the *type* of the moral law. In all of Kant's writings, this section of the *Critique of Practical Reason* contains the only such usage of "type."[3] A "type" is a posited natural law that functions as a kind of test for maxims adopted in nature, a test against the standard of the moral law. Suppose that each of the following is posited as a candidate for the status of natural law (i.e., a maxim applied *in concreto*): "it is permissible to deceive in order to gain advantage," or "it is permissible to end one's life when tired of it," or "it is permissible to regard the needs of others with indifference." All fail this test, although in fact each *can* be adopted. Their opposites (though Kant doesn't say so here) pass the test and so qualify as types of the moral law.[4]

What can be made of this ambivalence concerning the use of the word "schema" and of the apparent exclusion of imagination from the application of the moral law to the objects of nature? There is neither such ambiguity nor such exclusion in an early footnote in *Religion within the Limits of Reason Alone*. This note, presented as a response to Schiller,[5] connects the moral law, the idea of duty, and virtuous action: "If we consider . . . the happy results which virtue [i.e., the firmly grounded disposition strictly to fulfill our duty], should she gain admittance everywhere, would spread throughout the world, [we see] morally directed reason (by means of the imagination [*Einbildungskraft*]) calling sensibility into play" (VI, 23n). Here, imagination is declared to be precisely the means by which the moral law is enacted *in concreto*. At this juncture, it is necessary to recollect the ongoing essential *self-effacing* of imagination spoken of in the first Critique. Imagination is responsible for all synthesis but we are scarcely ever conscious of it.

How can these two quite disparate and apparently contradictory views be thought together, one expressly excluding imagination and the other expressly requiring imagination? I begin by attending carefully to Kant's language in the Typic: There can be no other mediating faculty *to an idea of reason* than the understanding. But this says nothing in principle other than what was said in the Deduction in the Dialectic of the *Critique of Pure Reason*. There, the idea served to unify the manifold of knowledge assembled under the categories of the pure understanding into a (practically necessary) system. Schematization occurred on a much more immediate level of the synthesis, in the application of the categories to (heterogeneous) intuition, as Kant notes here in the Typic. But, a synthesis of imagination must have already occurred. Thus, just as theoretical reason is brought to stand within the sway of transcendental imagination, so too is practical reason. The chart on the following page presents the analogy.

The difference between the two critiques that Kant attempts to sharpen in the Typic does not amount to very much once the internal workings of imagination are discerned. The principal difference between the two in terms of mediation is this: While all empirical intuitions presuppose pure intuition as determined by the categories and schemata, it is not the case that all actions in the world of sense occur as governed by universalizable maxims. However, in both cases, a synthesis of imagination generates the region within which what is proper to each (experience under rules and laws, moral actions under the idea of the moral law) can occur. And in both cases,

The Concept of an Object of Pure Practical Reason

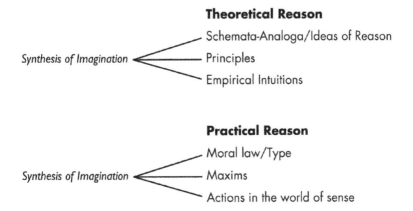

Theoretical Reason

Synthesis of Imagination
- Schemata-Analoga/Ideas of Reason
- Principles
- Empirical Intuitions

Practical Reason

Synthesis of Imagination
- Moral law/Type
- Maxims
- Actions in the world of sense

lawfulness is brought to this synthesis as a means of keeping human beings within the scope of its sway.

When these regions are regarded entirely in *conceptual* terms alone— i.e., once we suppose our knowledge of experience results from concepts rather than from the *synthesis* of concepts and their schemata, and once we suppose that from the concept of (unconditioned) freedom alone and not from the synthetic *a priori* form of a law that makes possible both maxim-formation and the application of maxims *in concreto*—reason falls prey to the various dangers delineated above. With respect to the *Critique of Practical Reason* just as much as with respect to the *Critique of Pure Reason*, the synthesis of imagination is at once productive and measuring.[6] It is only by bringing itself in the service of this synthesis that reason can truly fashion and enact a pure practical faculty that can at once serve as a standard and as a cause of action in accord with that standard. According to the architectural metaphor, the synthesis of imagination guided by reason provides the plan for the construction of a home appropriate to a human being.

The Incentives (*Triebfeder*) of Pure Practical Reason

Incentive-Creating Imagination and Moral Feeling

An incentive[1] is a subjective ground of the determination of the will. Clearly, only the moral law itself can qualify as a moral incentive in any sense, for it is the sole incentive that is also an *objective* determining ground of the will. The latter must be "the exclusive and subjectively sufficient determining ground of action if [the will] is to fulfill not only the *letter* of the law but its *spirit*" (V, 72, emphasis in original). This chapter yields a rich harvest from the synthesis of imagination.

First of all, imagination extends the moral law from its status as a pure form of a law in general and an "intellectual cause" to an actual incentive (*Triebfeder*), a drive at play with other drives. Secondly and quite strikingly, imagination brings this incentive into opposed play with the inclinations, all of which are thwarted by this clash. The result is pain. Kant notes that this is quite remarkable: an *a priori* concept capable of determining the feeling of pleasure and displeasure.[2] From the standpoint, however, of the *alreadiness* of the synthesis of imagination in every determination of the will, it is clear that the moral realm is always a realm of finite beings, and that competing images are at play. Here, the images are at play in the guise of incentives.

The Incentives (*Triebfeder*) of Pure Practical Reason

However play does not exclude seriousness at all. The play of incentives, by which I mean those incentives fashioned by a finite being in accord with this finite nature, is at once a battlefield. Enemies that can do various degrees of harm are found on this battlefield. Just as in the case of the "hypotheses at war," the principal battlefield is not external, but in us. Self-love or selfishness is one such enemy. This enemy is in us and cannot be totally extirpated. In a sense it is not simply an enemy; self-love causes us to direct ourselves toward our own happiness that can, after a fashion (as the Dialectic will demonstrate), conform to morality. Kant says that pure practical reason merely gives an interruption (*Abbruch tut*) to selfishness. Arrogance (*Selbstsucht*) is a more serious enemy, an enemy that pure practical reason beats down (*schlägt nieder*), for its propensity is "false and opposed to the law" (V, 73).

In this light, the notion that Kant is in any way oblivious to the pull of competing influences upon the human being, and that his moral philosophy fails to account for it, could not be more preposterous. The many dispositions that fall under the titles "*selfishness*" and "*arrogance*" populate the territory of human transgression in a thoroughgoing way. After explaining how the moral law is itself an incentive, that the interest attaching to it must be non-sensuous, and that genuine moral maxims must rest upon this interest, he writes that "[a]ll three concepts—of incentive, interest, and maxim—can, however, be applied only to finite beings" (V, 79). A divine will, good by its very nature, requires no incentives at all. Just as the divine intellect was said to have no need of thought since thought always involves limitations, the presence of incentives in the divine will would suggest limitation as well.

In terms of the structure of the *Critique of Practical Reason*, selfishness and arrogance make the intertwining of imagination and reason in their pure synthesis impossible. In actual deed, however, these motives commonly occur together. If this were the critique of theoretical reason, an experience that was not subject to the natural law of causality would be impossible both in thought *and* in deed. But in this critique of practical reason, while it is impossible to universalize one's maxims under either the more benign incentive of self-love or under the more malevolent incentive of arrogance, it is quite possible to form maxims in accord with these incentives, and to perform actions in accord with these maxims. Our freedom assures us of this ever-present, ever-dangerous possibility.

There is, however, one sense in which there really is no escaping the moral law for anyone. Just as the synthesis of imagination begets an incentive peculiar to morality, it also begets a feeling that attaches to pure practical reason alone. The moral feeling is unlike any other. It is a *pure feeling,* generated spontaneously from reason by imagination.[3] Like the incentives, moral feeling takes its place among the play of other feelings—a multifarious play indeed—but as a stranger to all of the others by virtue of its purity. However, the moral feeling is like the incentives in this sense, that *qua* feeling its presence is indisputable, however much a person may wish to deny it.

In this context, Kant cites Fontanelle, who said, "I bow to a great man, but my spirit does not bow," to which Kant adds "to a humble, plain (*bürgerlich gemein*) man, in whom I perceive righteousness to a higher degree than I am conscious of in myself, *my spirit bows* **whether I choose or not,** however high I carry my head that he may not forget my superior position" (V, 77, first emphasis in original, second emphasis mine). The power of moral feeling is like no other in that it can cause the kind of pain Kant calls *humiliation* (intellectual contempt) (*Demütigung* [*intellectuelle Verachtung*]). Far deeper than shame, the pain caused by the moral feeling addresses itself to the basic worth of my humanity. It compels me to accept the judgment that has produced this feeling: humiliation itself becomes disclosive of my moral nature. No pathological feeling, however painful, can serve to bring us on the path of self-reflection the way the moral feeling can.

Moral feeling, then, discloses our moral nature in the most positive sense possible. Kant calls this positive sense *"respect for the law,"* saying of respect that "it is not the incentive to morality. It is morality itself" (V, 76). But insofar as "morality itself" includes both moral law and moral feeling, morality by its nature presupposes the pure synthesis of imagination. Morality itself, then, takes place within the play of feelings that mark human nature. Once again, Kant affirms this nature. The play of feelings to which the moral feeling belongs among others is another way of saying what Kant acknowledges here and throughout: "it presupposes the sensuousness and hence the finitude of such beings on whom respect for the law is imposed" (V, 76).

Only in this way can sense be made of Kant's example of "the law made intuitable (*anschaulich*)" (V, 77). While the law itself works as an intelligible cause, the finite human being in whom it has taken hold in spirit serves as an *example* to me. Morality as the conjoining of the moral law and the moral feeling in respect presents an image so powerful that respect cannot be withheld. "[W]e can indeed outwardly withhold it, but we cannot help feeling (*empfinden*) it inwardly" (V, 77).

Kant has several formulations of respect for the law, every one of which indicates the prior synthesis of imagination. Subjectively, it is an incentive, generated by the bond of the moral law to moral feeling. He also calls it "a positive but indirect effect of the law on feeling" (V, 79). This indicates clearly that a *synthesis* is required between the law and feeling. He also calls it a particular act of the will, coupled with our awareness of this act: "The consciousness of a *free* submission of the will to the law, combined with the inevitable constraint imposed only by our own reason on all inclinations, is respect for the law" (V, 80, emphasis in original). In respect, then, the synthesis of imagination gathers lawfulness, feeling, and the realm of sensation (inclination) in a single and simultaneous act. I shall try to survey the Kantian edifice from this propitious point.

Earlier, freedom was said to serve as the cornerstone of the system of reason by virtue of its installation into the abyss at the heart of human nature by productive imagination. This abyss may be characterized in terms of radical absence, the absence of any knowledge of originals in the realm of theoretical knowledge, and the blindness to ourselves of both the dark source of the standard of moral judgments and even of our own motives when we strive to act in accord with that opaquely given but nevertheless binding standard. The moral law (the *ratio cognoscendi* of freedom, the pure form of giving universal law) was seen as that pure image of a rationally self-directing will supporting both its pursuit of truth and its pursuit of goodness. Freedom serves as a cornerstone, gathering them into a one, into a system. It is not an original, but belongs to the image-play that it serves. Not a single theoretical insight can be derived from it nor can a single action, although principles that govern their respective realms can surely be discerned. Freedom, then, was seen as bringing unity precisely by allowing for principles that leave the respective regions open to the play of images.

Can *respect*, which gathers together consciousness, the will, the moral law, moral feeling, and the inclinations serve as the keystone of the Kantian edifice? It would not seem so, since Kant says clearly that respect applies to persons and not to things, and since the inclinations are precisely excluded by respect. However, several considerations point in respect's direction. First, the *Critique of Pure Reason* excludes consideration of the will and the feeling of pleasure and pain (A49, B66) that are precisely the subject matter of the *Critique of Practical Reason* and the *Critique of Judgment* respectively.[4] Further and more deeply, this very exclusion is itself an act of the will, an act of practical reason. In this light, both the scrupulous effort to represent the nature and limits of reason in its truth, including the way in which truth enters into the theoretical framework, is ultimately a moral act. Since this act is an act of a being who is given over to feeling, it must somehow be given over first of all to the will and its attendant feeling in the moral realm, just as intuition constitutes immediate relation to an object in the theoretical realm.

Accordingly, sensuous intuition can be seen as a secondary manifestation of feeling, i.e., it can be seen as feeling with the moral and pathological content abstracted entirely from it. Only by abstracting from the swirl of feelings can nature be regarded as sensuous appearances conforming to the principles of understanding. Only by so abstracting, that is, can science be conducted. Thus, moral feeling can qualify as the keystone, both the high point and the ultimate support upon which the entire Kantian edifice rests. It extends often silently through moral actions to theoretical determinations.

The synthesis of imagination has produced a unified ruling image to which all humanity not only must assent, but already assents in some way (i.e., inwardly at the very least) whether it admits to this feeling or not.

In this light, the Typic can be seen as systematically prior to the Schematism to which Kant compared it in the section bearing its name. The type of a law, which Kant called a symbol rather than a schema, can be seen at once as a "higher level" schema, a representation that the synthesis of imagination produces in order to connect the moral law to nature and to effect its application to maxims consistent with universal laws. But in terms of the moral feeling in its capacity as keystone, the Typic is also the act of judgment that issues out of this feeling when the will wills an action in accord with the moral law. The Schematism, then, can be seen as abstracted from the Typic precisely as sensuous intuitions are abstracted from feelings. The lawfulness of all appearances, which is guaranteed by the relation to pure intuition of the schemata in the principles, can be seen as issuing from the restriction to the understanding and its objects (of intuition) by the *Critique of Pure Reason,* and from the conscious exclusion of the will and feeling—although, as has been shown, this is a *willful* exclusion.

Similarly, duty, which Kant calls the action arising from the aforementioned consciousness of the law and the exclusion of inclination, can be seen as the systematically prior manifestation of *truth* in the theoretical realm. Just as duty represents an action conformable to the conditions for its (moral) possibility, truth is—in general—a representation in conformity with the principles and with the intuitions to which they refer. The reason duty can be violated in two ways[5] while an empirical judgment can only be true or false[6] resides in the aforementioned abstraction of the theoretical realm from the practical. The realm of theoretical knowledge, with all its ever-ongoing richness, is in truth a subset of the practical realm in which the phenomena are flattened out; it is a realm in which the will and feeling are excluded from their consideration.

With the will and the moral law synthesized into their fullness in moral feeling, we are granted the vision of the origin in practical reason of the entire system of reason; this vision is given in the image of a *person*. One might call the invisible inner structure of the "law made visible in an example" mentioned above by the name *personality*. Kant presents a series of qualities according to which one can discern personhood in a genuinely moral sense. First of all, it disdains "exhortations to actions as noble, sublime and magnanimous" (V, 84–85), focusing only upon "obligation" (V, 85).

While disdaining those excessive incitements out of self-conceit, Kant does not hesitate to give his own apostrophe to duty. It is far less flowery in German than as generally rendered in English.[7] In this well-known passage, Kant ascribes a "sublime, great name" (V, 86) to it, but as an exclamatory event it is hardly disjoined from the rest of the text, for it concludes with a question: "what origin is worthy of you, and where is to be found the noble descent which proudly rejects all kinship with the inclinations and from which to be descended is the indispensable condition of the only worth that men can give themselves?" (V, 86).

In one word, *personality* is the origin. Packed into the notion of personality are virtually all the products of pure synthesis of imagination and pure images that I have been at pains to disclose as operative in the *Critique of Practical Reason* from the beginning of this text: autonomy, holiness, the principle of humanity, respect. Negatively, personality means "freedom and independence from the mechanism of nature" (V, 87). Affirmatively, it is the source from which all worth (*Werthe*) flows for a human being.

The addition of *sublimity* to this list requires some explanation. "We call that *sublime* which is *absolutely great*"[8] (V, 248). Not only is the notion that any human being is absolutely great preposterous, but almost as ridiculous is the notion that any human being can properly be called *great* at all. Both the inscrutability of the intentions of others and our own internal blindness prevent us from accepting this ascription. While "[m]an is certainly unholy enough, but humanity in his person must be holy to him" (V, 87), it is difficult to see how this finite humanity, even considered as autonomous, is sublime. I suggest that this sublimity is brought to an image in the notion of a *comfort* (*Trost*) that issues solely from the consciousness that one has "honored and preserved humanity in his own person and in its dignity" (V, 88), and that has nothing whatsoever to do with happiness and even with life.

What is this comfort that disdains happiness (*Glückseligkeit*) and life and all enjoyment (*Genuß*)? "Comfort" is misinterpreted entirely if it is seen as contempt for life. Rather, it must be seen as the drawing up of life in terms of the only image that can present this life as a fully human one, i.e., one that is conducted in accord with those supersensuous principles alone that are larger than life and awaken respect for the possibility of life given to us.[9] In a provocative choice of words, Kant writes that "the pure moral law itself *lets be traced* (*spüren lässt*) the sublimity of our own supersensuous existence and subjectively effects respect for [our] higher vocation" (V, 88). The peculiar supersensuous drawing of a pure image allows us at once to behold and to participate vicariously in an image of ourselves that provides appropriate measure for a human being. It shows us our calling and our capacity to answer that call, just as it wards off the self-conceit that would dishonor it.

Imagination at once synthesizes and produces images. Here, in the drawing of the pure image of the moral law so that our existence can be experienced as sublime, imagination redirects human mindfulness from the manifold and diffuse tendencies dictated by the natural inclination of happiness-seeking to the unity within ourselves that only the moral life can provide.[10] The power that generates both the moral law and its pure image remains concealed, its contribution unacknowledged, but its work clearly accomplished.

PART 2

Dialectic and Methodology of
Pure Practical Reason

FOUR

Dialectic of Pure Practical Reason in General and Imagination

A Dialectic of Pure Practical Reason in General

The short chapter with this particular title structures all that will follow. Its peculiar title signals its content: the phrase "a dialectic in general" refers to an unavoidable illusion that occurs when the bonds to the sensible condition to which we human beings are given over are transgressed, and reason strives to reach the unconditioned basis of all conditions. "A Dialectic of Pure Practical Reason" refers to that transgression insofar as it occurs in the pursuit of the good, just as a dialectic of pure (speculative, theoretical) reason refers to the transgression insofar as it occurs in the pursuit of the true.

Just as the theoretical dialectic departs from the bond to intuition, attempting to transcend this bond in order to achieve knowledge of the soul, the world, and God as they are in themselves, the practical dialectic takes its departure from "the practically conditioned (which rests upon inclinations and natural need)" (V, 108). The "thing in itself" to which our practical condition extends in the dialectic is the *highest good*.

The analogy to the extension in the dialectic of theoretical reason is clear. In theoretical reason, our fragmented intuitions are brought to the unity of the pure concepts of understanding by means of the synthesis of imagination. In practical reason, our inclinations and natural needs are brought to unity under the categories governed by the moral law as an "ought," with imagination effecting the mediation between the pure moral law and its application *in concreto* (as shown in the section on the Typic above).

And just as the extension of the pure concepts of the understanding by imagination beyond the bond to intuition that gives them sense and significance yields the illusory knowledge of the soul, the world, and God—supposedly the highest source(s) of *truth*—the extension of the moral law beyond its bond to human needfulness to its object, the highest *good*, yields the illusion that one has found the unconditional determining ground of the pure will.

The key passage in this section is the parenthetical one noted above: "the practically conditioned (which rests upon inclinations and natural needs)." That is to say, human finitude provides both the forgotten ground that allows for the Dialectic of Pure Practical Reason to develop, and the recollected basis for its solution.

The Dialectic of Pure Reason in Defining the Highest Good

The bond of the concept of the highest good to human finitude is established in the opening paragraph of this section. While virtue as worthiness to be happy is the highest good insofar as it is the supreme good (*das Oberste*), it is "not by itself the entire or complete good (*das ganze or vollendete Gut*)" (V, 110). Kant explains that the faculty of desire in a finite rational being requires the addition of happiness to virtue—in proportion to one's worthiness.

Disputing the view of the ancients (as he interprets it) that morality and happiness are two aspects of the highest good and therefore are its (logically analytic) predicates, Kant insists on the heterogeneity of these two components. He notes instead that far from being component "predicates" of the highest good, morality and happiness "strongly limit and check each other in the same subject" (V, 112). Hence, the highest good contains a *synthesis* of concepts. He maintains that this synthesis is cognized *a priori*, and so requires a transcendental deduction. As has been often noted, synthesis is the work of imagination, which also fashions images in its act of synthesis. The question is now: How can such a deduction occur in the case of the highest good?

A transcendental (objective) deduction is "[t]he explanation of the manner in which concepts can thus relate *a priori* to objects" (A85, B117). The highest good is the "entire *object* of a pure practical reason" (V, 109). Thus, its possibility must be deduced from its component heterogeneous concepts. Nowhere does Kant mention imagination in this deduction. In fact, he does not mention the word "deduction" after announcing that one is required! Yet imagination is fully at work within the promised and enacted but unmentioned deduction.

How can two determinations that check and limit one another such as morality and happiness be deduced in such a way that they relate *a priori* to the highest good? Earlier in this section, Kant claimed that "two determinations (*Bestimmungen*) necessarily combined in one concept must be related as ground and consequent" (V, 111). Of the two possible connections, it is clear from the Analytic that only the one according to which virtue is the ground of happiness can qualify as the synthesis that produces the highest good. But given the two mutually limiting determinations, there is nothing to prohibit imagination from effecting that synthesis in the opposite manner. Indeed, this is precisely the synthesis that (unconsciously) occurs whenever one acts from the motive of self-love with the aim of achieving happiness.[1]

This absence of prohibition, however, is merely another way of understanding freedom in the sense of choice (*Willkür*). This sense is merely a shadow of the full sense of freedom as autonomy.[2] But freedom is the necessarily asserted ground of the synthesis. Happiness, then, must be its consequent. The problem belonging to this deduction is analogous to the problem belonging to the prior deductions in this sense: How can the spontaneously generated cognition (in this case, the conception of the moral law as the *ratio cognoscendi* of freedom) serve as the ground of the heterogeneous (and, in light of human nature, receptive) concept of happiness?

In subsection I, "The Antinomy of Practical Reason," Kant sets the problem: Since the two spheres of causality (i.e., of freedom and of nature) are heterogeneous, it seems that there can be no necessary connection between them. Therefore, the highest good, which is the necessary object of our will, is impossible. Ultimately, then, the moral law must itself be "fantastic, directed toward imaginary (*eingebildete*) purposes, and thus false in itself" (V, 114). The moral law would be "false in itself" because truth, even in its most minimal sense for Kant, requires the agreement of a cognition—in this case the moral law as the law of our will—with its object, here the highest good (A58, B83).

Since synthesis is the work of imagination, any connection between the moral law and the highest good must be effected by imagination. However, the "purposes" toward which the synthesis is directed must be bound to human nature in its finitude. Much as the syntheses of imagination in the *Critique of Pure Reason* directed themselves to human finitude as made manifest in the bond to sensible intuition, the synthesis of imagination in the *Critique of Practical Reason* will be directed toward the bond of human desire toward happiness.

In subsection II, the resolution of the Antinomy is presented, a resolution that resembles the resolutions of the antinomies in the *Critique of Pure Reason*, although it is not quite isomorphic with them.[3] While it is absolutely false that happiness is the ground of morality, it is only conditionally false that morality can be the ground of happiness. That condition, of course, is the restriction of causality to the world of sense. Assuming an intelligible causality—the basic assumption and assertion of the entire Kantian practical philosophy!— there is no impossibility in the moral antinomy just as there is none in the theoretical antinomy.[4]

The synthesis in the *Critique of Practical Reason* is far bolder than any in the *Critique of Pure Reason*. In the *Critique of Pure Reason*, Kant connects the possible *intelligible* "I" as cause of my actions in the sensible world to the *sensible* "I" as subject to natural causality by maintaining that it is not a contradiction for the two causalities to coexist. In other words, he makes the modest claim that there is a possible synthesis of sensible and intelligible causality. Nothing is said concerning what might constitute a mediating representation of such a synthesis. In the *Critique of Practical Reason*, the mediating representation is clearly spelled out. Since one cannot hope for a direct ground/consequence relation between morality and happiness in this life, "this relation is indirect (mediated by an intelligible originator (*Urheber*) of nature . . .)" (V, 115).

What can be the source of such a being? Kant has ruled out any theological basis for morality. In the Ideal of Pure Reason of the *Critique of Pure Reason*, any attempt to prove the existence of such a being was shown to rest upon the ontological argument, and this argument was shown to be invalid on account of its mistaken assumption that existence is a real predicate. Nevertheless, any and all ideas of God are mere extensions by imagination of the pure concept of Community to the unconditioned. So this particular idea (i.e., originator) is a product of imagination. So too is the *connection* (*Verknüpfung*) between morality and happiness that Kant examines in this section. He finds that it must be strange (*befremden*) that both ancients and moderns have, on various accounts, linked morality and happiness in *this* life.

His criticisms issue one and all from insight into the heterogeneity of morality and happiness. Both the tendency of a finite being (1) to regard them as directly related (as the Epicureans and Stoics did, although in different ways) and/or (2) to mistake one's own motives such that feelings of moral worth (which are often illusory) are improperly regarded as the ground of happiness, issue from the confounding of the realms from which they respectively derive. In this life, one cannot properly link morality and happiness as ground and consequent. A daring act of imagination, out of which a future life is fashioned, is required to justify their link at all.

What can properly be said about the adumbrated "next life" or "other life" in an intelligible world? Just as in the case of the theoretical antinomy of freedom and natural causality, it is at least non-contradictory to posit such a notion. But once again, the representation of such a world is bolder and richer still than the positing of an intelligible "I" as member of an intelligible world. Here, there is a connection between morality (as worthiness to be happy) and happiness such that the latter is *exactly* proportioned to the former. This exact proportionality is required for the truth of the moral law, namely that it correspond to its object, the highest good.

But this means the following: Truth here is made possible by the synthesis of imagination, which brings "the next life" into being as a *pure image*. "The next life" functions, then, much as a schema of an idea of pure reason does. In the latter, as has been claimed, the schema of a concept of a thing in general (A607, B698) served to allow the empirical manifold to be brought by imagination under the unity of an idea. Here, the "schema-analogon" of "the next life" allows the manifold of the satisfaction of human desires to be brought to (proportionate) unity under the moral law.[5]

As to this life, Kant speaks of an "analogon of happiness" which is called self-satisfaction (*Selbstzufriedenheit*). He also calls it "negative pleasure (*Wohlgefallen*) with one's existence" and "intellectual satisfaction" (all V, 117–18). All these formulations indicate an independence from inclinations. Inclinations, even the best-natured ones, are called "burdensome to a rational being," and "blind and slavish." Kant makes what seems to be the extraordinary claim that a rational being wishes "to be relieved of them" (all V, 118). Given that our finite nature is made manifest in needs and inclinations, given further that their satisfaction is taken by us to be happiness, and recalling that happiness is one component of the highest good, how can one understand Kant's comments that these needs and inclinations are one and all burdensome and contemptible? Must it be concluded that a hatred of our finitude informs Kant's moral vision?

I strongly maintain that no such interpretation is sustainable. The issue does not concern happiness as the mere satisfaction of pathological desires at all. Nor does it concern happiness as it might pertain to a rational being with no needs at all, i.e., to an infinite being (if indeed it makes sense at all to speak of the happiness of such a being). Rather, Kant is concerned to show precisely what sort of happiness accords with a being (ourselves) whose nature is both rational and pathological. To such a being, *only* a happiness in proportion to one's moral worth has sense and significance. And such proportionality can only be projected into the next life.

The self-satisfaction in this life, then, images that intelligible proportionality. The "negative pleasure" it brings is ultimately affirmative, for it serves to keep the human being alertly attending to the power to distance herself or himself from inclinations. In this context, all inclinations and needs are disturbances and intrusions upon the effort to fashion one's actions from duty alone, which is the only way to achieve the self-satisfaction that is this life's surrogate for happiness. In terms of the *pure* synthesis of imagination, (intelligible) morality cannot cross into the heterogeneous realm of (sensuous) happiness. Only a synthesis that yields an intelligible analogue of the moral law can satisfy the requirements of a finite rational being of needs. This synthesis, then, must be one that both abstracts entirely from those needs in determining the maxim of action and that takes satisfaction from so acting.

One might recall the opening of Book V of Plato's *Republic,* where Adiemantus challenges Socrates on the issue of the happiness of the guardians. In return for their noble service to the city, they seem to receive nothing. They own nothing, and they live in a very austere manner—so how can they be called happy? Socrates replies that while they would not have the happiness of those who feast and enjoy material comforts, they would have a happiness that accords with their nature as guardians. He distinguishes this from the adolescent conception of happiness that most people seem to hold. While the analogy to Kant's view is not precise, it is nevertheless quite suggestive. Just as the self-examination and self-censure spoken of above takes place on an entirely different level than that of the satisfaction of pathological desires and according to an entirely different measure, so here the pursuit of happiness takes place in accord with a standard quite other than the one held by *hoi polloi.* Kant is speaking precisely of a happiness that accords with human nature as rational. This happiness—self-satisfaction—is the result of the synthesis of imagination connecting an action done from duty with the contentment that comes with the awareness that one has so acted.

On the Primacy of Practical Reason in Its Association with Speculative Reason

The placement of this section follows the pattern of the *Critique of Pure Reason* in the sense that after the antinomy of reason is resolved a discussion of the *interests* of reason follows. Just as in the first critique, the resolution of the antinomy of pure practical reason involves the *possibility* of a synthetic principle that transcends natural causality. The assertion of this possibility occurs on the basis of what Kant calls an *interest*, which is always an interest of a finite being. The theses and antitheses of the four antinomies of pure (speculative) reason found two different interested parties (perhaps contestants within the same mind!) vouching for them, rationalists for the former, empiricists for the latter. For the former, the theses (which Kant called the "dogmatism of pure reason") answered a certain comfort and general practical interest, but undermined the epistemological interest in adhering to the evidence of experience. For the latter, the antitheses provided sure epistemological guidance but undermined the practical interest when they functioned dogmatically. Apart from any interest, however, there is nothing to choose between them. More pitifully even than Buridan's ass, human beings would vacillate endlessly and pointlessly between thesis and antithesis.

Yet one must choose, and Kant writes, "[I]f, however they were summoned to action, this play of merely speculative reason would, like a dream, at once cease, and they would choose their principles exclusively in accordance with practical interests" (A475, B503). Thus, the subordination of theoretical principles to practical ones can be said to arise from the negative nature of theoretical knowledge of the ideas, which would freeze all action by virtue of the conflict of speculative reason with itself. In the *Critique of Practical Reason*, the primacy of the practical is presented in a positive light: "if pure reason really is practical, as the consciousness of the moral law shows it to be, it is only one and the same reason which judges *a priori* by principles, whether for theoretical or practical purposes" (V, 121).

To "judge *a priori*" means to enact the entire spontaneous apparatus. One could well say that this very enactment implies the primacy of practical reason, since reason itself is first and foremost an *act*, whether it addresses itself to the will and its choice of maxims or to the understanding in its empirical employment. But this section claims that the primacy is determined by propositions "belonging imprescriptibly to the practical interest of pure reason" and "indeed as something grown from outside and not grown it its own soil" (V, 121).

Clearly, these propositions are the moral law and the maxims in accord with it. Where, then, are these practical propositions grown?

Kant calls them "extensions" (*Erweiterungen*) of pure reason's use, serving the interest of pure reason by preventing speculative folly. As shown earlier, such extensions are one and all the work of imagination. However, while the extensions on the side of theoretical reason lead to the aforementioned undecidability, i.e., to the inability of reason to choose and so to act, this extension of reason's use has precisely the opposite effect: it brings a principle to reason such that reason *must* act, and must act in a certain way. In other words (and in the language of the *Foundations*), the will is (pure) practical reason itself. But where is this "*outside*" of pure reason as the source of this principle? It is nothing other than the fact of freedom. This fact is asserted, but its reality cannot be proven by theoretical reason alone.

Since the principle governing all practical propositions is founded on the fact of freedom, and the synthesis of imagination is responsible for the extension of reason beyond the limits of speculation, the primacy of practical reason is a function of imagination's fashioning the whole of reason as an *image of freedom*. This also means the following: As one who acts and must act, and as one to whom the principle of action is always present, the human being has been granted the possibility of a life of dignity. Such a life directs itself by choosing maxims in accord with the moral law from duty. Such a life is also proscribed from acting out of the conceit that one has knowledge of those basic concerns of God, freedom, and immortality (Kant's "speculative folly") when such knowledge is closed off from humanity.

The choosing of maxims in accord with the moral law is itself a synthesis of imagination, as has been seen, whereby the pure form of a law in general is concretized. The "I judge" presupposes such a synthesis in any case (theoretical or practical). The avoidance of speculative folly is a result of the same synthesis, but also involves the other side of imagination's work, namely its fashioning of *images*.

Whether it is theoretical or practical, the synthesis also involves the production of (pure or empirical) images. Both from the standpoint of self-knowledge (here, motives of our actions) and from that of the actions themselves, there can only be second-order knowledge. Like Socrates in the *Phaedo* who recognizes that knowledge of ultimate causes cannot be achieved and so sets out on a course that is "second-best" but worthy, in Kant's thought the human actor is granted a pathway to right action while holding this actor within appropriate limits.

Kant concludes this section by noting that "every interest is ultimately practical" (V, 121). While the primacy of practical reason can at least nominally follow from this insight and can follow more substantively from the need to resolve the otherwise ever-contested antinomies for the sake of the possibility of meaningful action, the concealed but ever-present work of imagination provides a more originary sense of this primacy. Recalling A78, B103 of the *Critique of Pure Reason*, synthesis is said to be "the mere effect (*Wirkung*) of the power of imagination, a blind but indispensable function of the soul, without which we should have no knowledge whatsoever (*gar keine Erkenntnis haben würden*)." There, imagination seems to be spoken of in the language of *causality:* synthesis is the *effect* of which imagination is somehow the dimly and rarely glimpsed but indispensable *cause*.

Matters thicken further, of course, when one notes that imagination is required to unite the category of causality with (pure) intuition, thereby giving it meaning and significance (*Sinn und Bedeutung*) by virtue of its (the category's) schematization. However, when imagination is understood as *ever self-effacing act,* always present whether the human being thinks for the sake of discovering truth or wills (chooses maxims) for the sake of goodness, one can begin to see through these thickets as well as one can.

Imagination by itself (if it makes sense to speak in this way) is blind. Just as the categories give it eyes on the side of understanding, freedom gives it eyes on the side of the will. Insofar as human beings must always think of themselves as free subjects in the moral world, and therefore as their actions—whether those that are most common in everyday life or at the height of learned research—are one and all subject to inspection by the same moral law as the *ratio cognoscendi* of freedom, pure practical reason always has primacy over the speculative.

But since imagination drives all synthesis and therefore all rational activity, the primacy of the practical is ultimately . . . the primacy of imagination.

Imagination and the Postulates of Immortality and God

Kant's employment of the term "postulate" here coheres with its use in the *Critique of Pure Reason*. There, after distinguishing his use from the use to which the term is put by mathematicians (i.e., as intuitively certain propositions), he writes, "[postulates] do not increase our concept of things, but only show the manner in which it is connected with the faculty of knowledge" (A234–35, B287). In the realm of practical reason, where there is no extension of knowledge but rather an extension of reason's use, postulates attach to this practical use in an analogous way: "By a **postulate** of pure practical reason, I understand a *theoretical* proposition which is not as such demonstrable, but which is an inseparable corollary of (*unzertrennlich anhängt*) an *a priori* unconditionally valid *practical* law" (V, 122, emphases in original).

How must "theoretical" be interpreted in this context?

Clearly, it cannot mean "logical" in any narrow sense; in no way can the immortality of the soul (or the existence of God) be conceptually or inferentially derivable from the moral law. Even "transcendental-logical" must fall short; the schematized categories are one and all time-bound, and the very nature of the practical postulates frees them from any temporal condition. The Canon of Pure Reason in the *Critique of Pure Reason* provides a clue to the role of the theoretical postulates of immortality and God. The conviction one holds "is not *logical* but *moral* certainty; and since it rests on subjective grounds (of the moral sentiment), I must not even say, *it is* morally certain that there is a God, etc., but *'I am* morally certain, etc.'" (A829, B857).

That is to say, the propositions asserting the immortality of the soul and the existence of God receive their theoretical justification *through my act of freedom.* By virtue of my inserting myself into the command of the moral law and to the commitment to the highest good that this command entails, those propositions that produce dialectical illusion in pure theoretical reason receive their anchoring truth in practical reason through their inseparable bond with the moral law. This anchoring moral truth is hardly any comfort to anyone who regards the continuance of mere life to be a good in itself. Rather, it merely holds out the hope that one can continue to make moral progress beyond this life and so approach the goal of holiness that resides beyond our grasp in this life and, for Kant, in any other.[1]

The postulate of immortality is treated first, as it conforms to the portion of morality ("the first and principal part"—V, 124) belonging to the highest good. It is followed by the postulate of happiness, the highest good's other portion. Regarded epistemologically, they are necessary beliefs that attach to the moral law. Before exploring the technical aspect of the postulate of immortality, another Socratic comparison suggests itself here, namely an analogy with Socrates facing death in the *Apology.* At the conclusion of the Canon, Kant notes, "But, it will be said, is this all that pure reason achieves in opening up prospects beyond the limits of experience? Nothing more than two articles of belief (*Glaubensartikel*)? Surely the common understanding could have achieved as much, without appealing to the philosophers for counsel" (A830–31, B858–59). While once again the parallel is not exact, this result strongly suggests Socrates' fearlessness in the face of death as presented in Plato's *Apology,* as well as his insistent claim that he knows nothing worth knowing. This ignorance clearly extends to the reality of a future life. And while the treatments of immortality are arguably quite different,[2] Socrates' looking forward to the possibility of interrogating the heroes and the "true judges" in Hades (41a) in order to discover the best life for a human being can be seen as imaging the Kantian ongoing quest for a moral life that would be worthy of the greatest happiness.

Kant writes of the human being's ongoing progress that "he cannot hope here or at any foreseeable point of his future existence to be fully adequate to God's will, without indulgence or remission which would not harmonize with justice. This he can do only in the infinity of his duration which God alone can survey" (V, 124–25). On one hand, this can be read as the bleakest of prospects. The conviction that one has an immortal soul condemns one to repeated frustration, condemns one to efforts that not only will likely fall short but are in principle incapable of ultimate success, however well-motivated. The postulate itself seems designed merely to fill a blank in the system; *some* sort of success must be postulated in order to satisfy reason's "ought implies can" requirement.

However, once again the Kantian moral philosophy must be read as prescribing an entirely different measure than one belonging to any kind of consequentialism, utilitarianism, eudaimonism, or theologism. Falling short morally is no occasion for self-flagellation. Rather, the choice of membership in a moral realm holds open not only a pathway to a life of dignity, but to the only possibility of a happiness suitable to finite beings like ourselves. To say, then, that I am morally certain of the immortality of my soul is to say nothing other than that I have chosen the moral realm as my own and so seek a dignified happiness, one that is proportionate to my desert. Recalling Socrates' final speech to those who voted for his acquittal, a life questioning the souls in Hades would be "happiest of all" (41c). But this life of questioning is precisely the way of his life on the earth.

From a technical standpoint, to say "I am morally certain of the immortality of the soul" is to say that I synthesize this proposition with the moral law to which I have already freely subjected myself. And that is to say that imagination has once again conjoined two propositions of differing contents. But just as in the case of the moral law, in which a twofold synthesis is always already operative (namely, the synthesis that begets the moral law itself and the synthesis that makes possible its application *in concreto* by means of maxims), a twofold synthesis is always already at work in the postulate of immortality.

This synthesis gathers the intentions of my actions in such a way that makes it possible for me, in my self-examination, to discern progress from worse in the past to better (but still flawed) in the present, and to project such progress as ongoing into a future life. I know no more about my soul than I did at the conclusion of the *Critique of Pure Reason*. My actions are still one and all appearances, which I subject to an intelligible cause by an act of freedom that occurs by virtue of a law prescribed from outside the theoretical realm. But the postulate of immortality holds open that play-space of a future life where what I have learned through my self-examination and achieved by means of redirecting my actions in terms of such reflection can continue to enable me to progress. For one who accepts this measure, perhaps even a certain cheerfulness is built into the imaginative synthesis that produces it.

The Existence of God as a Postulate of Pure Practical Reason

The postulate of the existence of God belongs to the opening up of that same play-space, here providing for the possibility of happiness by postulating "the existence . . . of a cause of the whole of nature, itself distinct from nature, which contains the ground of the exact coincidence (*Übereinstimmung*) of happiness with morality" (V, 125).

Like the postulate of immortality, the postulate of God is not itself duty, but issues from the duty to further the highest good—with the latter requiring the proportionate intersection of morality and happiness, an intersection that cannot be vouchsafed in this life, i.e., in the sensible region.

As was established in the treatment of Section II, the Antinomy of Pure Practical Reason in Defining the Highest Good, the notion of a "next life" in which this proportionate intersection could occur is the product of a synthesis of imagination that begets a pure image. The highest good is nothing other than that pure image of proportionate intersection. However, it must be recalled—it must *always* be recalled—that the synthesis itself is the work of a finite being, a being of needs. Once the moral life is chosen, the idea of the possibility of infinite moral progress is one of those needs, and the idea of a proportionate happiness is another. There is nothing arbitrary about these needs, which are rooted in the nature of reason itself just as firmly as the need for an ungrounded happiness is a need connected with our pathological nature.

In this section, Kant recalls his earlier criticisms of the Epicurean and Stoic views, reminding of the former's mistaken grounding of morality in happiness and the latter's mistaken belief that moral virtue was completely attainable in this life. The Christian religion receives far more favorable treatment, as it seems to conform to the view that God is not an object of knowledge but of faith, that our motives can never be equal to the idea of morality in this life, and that a proper happiness in possible only in "the kingdom of God" where it is meted out appropriately. However, it is clear (or should be) that the moral law and the postulates are the measuring ground of the Christian religion, and that few of its exponents would regard God as the second of two postulates attaching to a prior ground, namely the moral law.

However, Kant does claim without any qualification that "through the concept of the highest good as the object and final end of pure practical reason, the moral law leads to religion." Religion "is the *knowledge* or *cognition* (*Erkenntnis*) *of all duties as divine commands*" (V, 129, emphases in original), not as arbitrary sanctions but as "essential *laws*" of every free will. In what sense can religion be called "knowledge"? And what can be made of the phrase "*knowledge* of all duties as divine commands," especially given that the Kantian God is ruled out utterly as the ground of that morality, is never said to speak at all, and serves merely as the intelligible ground of the possible union of morality and happiness?

The key word in this passage is, I suggest, the "*as.*" The relationship of duties to a commanding divinity is an *analogical* one, having no justification in theoretical reason since we can have no knowledge of a (in principle non-appearing) God. Nor is there even any justification in terms of practical reason, which is restricted to freedom/ the moral law and the pursuit of the highest good and so require no commanding God. Kant says that the pursuit of the highest good *"leads to (führt)* religion," which is not the same as saying that it "implies" or is in any sense "necessarily connected with" religion. Further, the religion that Kant here expounds is said to be "disinterested *(uneigennützig),"* free of fear and hope as incentives (V, 129). A most peculiar religion indeed![3]

I suggest that *führen* here can refer only to a realm that is silently present though unaccounted for in the critical philosophy thus far. Namely, just as the human being as unique phenomenon occurs as an aesthetic act of freedom, i.e., as an image of freedom from which the original is withheld, the religion to which such a human being is led by virtue of her or his orientation to the highest good is an *aesthetic religion,* from which the original is withheld as well.[4]

This withholding can be regarded in two ways. First, both freedom and God are unknown. Second, even under the justified assertion of their reality, both moral and divine intentions are in some sense dark, inscrutable. Both the individual human being as an image of freedom and religion as the knowledge of duties as divine commands are *creations.* They are acts of imagination that introduce works that exceed the means of their production, i.e., they exceed the resources of both theoretical and practical reason that supposedly are the only sources capable of giving rise to them.

In this sense, Kant's treatment of religion in general, and of the Christian religion in particular, recalls in its own way the Greek experience of the gods, however much it differs in the particulars of belief (and however mortifying Kant might have found the comparison).[5] As much as the playful arbitrariness of the Greek gods may differ from the justice and mercy of the Christian God, the human being finds herself or himself fashioning a life regioned into a play-space that was not chosen. The task is to take up one's actions within that play-space in an appropriately human way, directing oneself toward what is best. For Kant, the moral law provides the measure and the highest good is the goal. For Socrates, the measure is the recognition of ignorance, the goal is action in a way that pleases the gods.

In terms of the Kantian philosophy (just as, in another way, in terms of the Platonic philosophy), this self-creation and self-orientation—both fashioned out of what is given—is the work of imagination. But the exposition of this kinship must await another occasion.

On the Postulates of Pure Practical Reason in General

This brief section solidifies the technical issues raised in the prior two sections. By virtue of the postulates, the ideas of the soul and of God that produced illusion in the realm of theory now find "objective reality" (V, 132) in the practical realm. Our knowledge (*Erkenntnis*) of them is therefore widened (*erweitert*), but only in a practical sense. It is widened by means of its connection with the moral law, which itself derives from the fact of freedom. "But how freedom is possible, and how we should think theoretically and positively of this type of causality, is not thereby discovered" (V, 133).

The widening of this knowledge cannot be the work of reason or of sense, but only of imagination extending the idea of freedom to the two components of the highest good not contained in that idea, but necessary for its fulfillment. Pure synthesis is always the work of imagination, which cannot be denied its powerful and central role in the *Critique of Practical Reason* even when it is not mentioned at all.

Imagination and the Moral Extension of Reason

How Is It Possible to Think (*Denken*) of Extending
Pure Reason in a Practical Respect Without Thereby
Extending Its Knowledge as Speculative?

It is clearly possible in a formal-logical sense to think the extension spoken of in the title to this section. Mere non-contradiction is sufficient for the thinkability of any proposition (Bxxvin). However, the question concerns possibility in a transcendental-logical sense, i.e., as pertaining *a priori* to the possibility of experience. Clearly, only propositions including a relation to intuition qualify. The Principles of Pure Reason are the ultimate ones as both *a priori* and synthetic.

Kant gives a somewhat surprising and convoluted answer to the question posed in the title of this section. He claims first that by asserting the reality of the ideas of reason in order to render them suitable for employment by pure practical reason, "no synthetic proposition is made possible by conceding their reality" (V, 134). Further, he claims that the three ideas "are not in themselves cognitions (*sind noch nicht an sich Erkenntnisse*)," though they are "transcendent thoughts in which there is nothing *impossible*" (V, 135, emphasis mine). Practically, it can be shown that they have objects, by virtue of their having been asserted as belonging to the concept of the highest good. However, "this, too, is not yet knowledge of *these objects;* for one can neither make synthetic judgments about them nor theoretically determine their application" (V, 135, emphasis in original).

A way to approach these puzzling claims can be located in the final paragraphs of this section, where Kant recalls the importance of the "laborious deduction of the categories" in the *Critique of Pure Reason*. This deduction, in establishing their *a priori* source in pure understanding but restricting their employment to objects of sensuous intuition ("empirical objects"), introduces that "*relation of balance* wherein reason in general can be purposefully used" (V, 141, emphasis in original). Our theoretical knowledge is restricted to objects as they appear. By virtue of our extension of the *a priori* concepts of understanding to the ideas, we may further "have *definite thoughts* about the *supersensuous* when applied to an object given by pure practical reason" (V, 141, emphases in original) and so locate the "path of wisdom" (V, 141).

Yet one cannot help but note the ambiguity and the consequent tension with which Kant is wrestling in the notion of knowledge (*Erkenntnis*) and of synthesis. At times he asserts that they belong to the practical realm. At other times he denies their belonging to it. The questions one must raise here are vexing. How, for example, can religion provide knowledge of duties as divine commands when there is no knowledge of God? How can the ideas associated with the highest good not admit of the possibility of synthesis when the highest good is itself said to be the outcome of a synthesis?

Perhaps it might be argued that, granting the antecedent presupposition of God's existence and of the synthesis belonging to the highest good, religion can properly be called a kind of knowledge and properly claim that the ideas of the soul and God are incapable subsequently of yielding synthetic propositions. But isn't it clearly fallacious to derive knowledge from belief, or doesn't this derivation require at least some explanation? And aren't "the soul is immortal" and "God exists" synthetic propositions by their very nature, wherever they occur and whatever their epistemological status?

According to the interpretation offered here, there is no escape from this ambiguity and from its attendant difficulties. For this ambiguity is nothing other than the one that haunts and that empowers the entire critical philosophy, namely the play of imagination and understanding. Strictly speaking—speaking, that is, according to the strictures established by the transcendental deduction of the categories to which Kant here appeals—there is nothing in the practical realm that can properly be called knowledge, and those judgments associated with the ideas are one and all synthetic. Practical "knowledge" and the ideas as "non-synthesizable elements" of the highest good gain "sense and significance" through that extension of the categories of understanding by imagination as they attach to the assertion of the fact of freedom.

Kant denies that the categories are either "inborn," a view he (mistakenly) attributes to Plato, nor acquired, a view he attributes to Epicurus.[1] Here in the text of the second critique he locates them in the pure understanding, as he has for the most part in the first critique. But clearly not until the categories are connected with the pure figurative synthesis of imagination, and ultimately with the schemata, do they acquire "sense and significance." Thus the balance that renders reason suitable for (theoretical) use is possible only through the twofold work of imagination: as synthesizing, in order to make experience possible at all, and as making images (understood here as objects of sense from which original insight is absent), to which all our knowledge is restricted.

Imagination's work in practical reason involves syntheses as well, but these are syntheses begetting images that have no correlate in experience at all. I have called them *pure images* for that reason. They are distinguished from the pure images belonging to theoretical reason in that they serve as vicarious images for action[2] and for a certain kind of life, but make no knowledge (strictly speaking) possible. As practical, however, these images direct all desire for knowledge. Freedom, as that image that grounds the other two ideas as the object (highest good) of all rational human striving, is therefore the keystone of the system of reason itself, bringing theoretical reason in service to life.

In his texts, Kant presents the theoretical realm primarily—and the practical realm virtually always—in terms of understanding and reason. Imagination, however, drives both realms.

Dialectic and Methodology of Pure Practical Reason

On Assent (*Fürwahrhalten*) Arising from a Need of Reason

Kant restates the difference between answering a need of theoretical and of practical reason. The need of the former for absolute completeness in the series of conditions, by virtue of its restriction to the sensible condition, cannot be met appropriately.[3] The need of the latter presents itself as a duty, i.e., as obliged by the moral law. As such, it is bound by no such restriction. This need is precisely the belief that the highest good is attainable, a belief that Kant calls by the admittedly unusual term "pure practical belief-in-reason" (*reine praktische Vernunftglauben*) (V, 144).

I ask, then, if assent, i.e., if "holding for true" issues from a *need* of reason, what must be concluded about this "truth"? Since this need is necessary belief grounded in the moral law but extending into the next life concerning which nothing, strictly speaking, is known, the correspondence of pure practical faith to the highest good must be a correspondence produced entirely by imagination.

Kant recognizes that "our reason finds it *impossible for it* to conceive, in the mere course of nature, a connection exactly proportioned and so thoroughly adapted to an end between natural events which occur according to laws [i.e., governing morality and governing pathological happiness] so heterogeneous" (V, 145, emphasis in original). However, this proportionality cannot be shown by theoretical reason to be impossible either. Into this breach—or more precisely, always already ahead of it—steps imagination in its capacity to fashion pure productive syntheses.

In the final paragraph of this section, Kant comments upon the voluntary (*freiwillige*) nature of pure rational faith, which he characterizes as "a decision (*Bestimmung*) . . . of our judgment (*unseres Urteils*) to assume that existence" (V, 146). What does *Freiheit* mean in this context? It cannot refer simply to the fact of freedom as *ratio essendi* of the moral law for the following reason: Insofar as assent to the highest good is a duty, it issues from the very moral law that expresses the fact of freedom. The need for this belief, Kant says, is a necessary need. It is at least very difficult to detach it from the moral law itself. The freedom of our judgment must refer to a sense of freedom in excess of moral freedom, one that makes moral freedom itself possible. It is freedom as the creative act of imagination, that act that silently undergirds the entire critical philosophy as it continually effaces itself.

On the Wise Adaptation of Man's Cognitive Faculties to His Practical Vocation (*Von der der praktischen Bestimmung des Menschens weislich angemessenes Proportionen sener Erkenntnisvermögen*)

Kant claims in this section that if reason's questions concerning the supersensible could be answered, not only would moral action be impossible (as human action would always be subject to an external measure, such as fear of *"God* and *eternity* in their *fearful majesty"* — V, 147), but also life itself would be meaningless. "The conduct of man . . . would be changed into a mere mechanism where, as in a puppet show, everything would gesticulate well but no life would be found in the figures" (V, 147).

Thus, the very withholding of this original knowledge is precisely what gives life meaning. We humans have only "a weak glimpse" of the supersensuous. A "disinterested respect" for the moral law is therefore commanded. At stake is the person and her or his intentions, not "interested" actions that might receive reward from a God that is somehow present. We humans must insert ourselves in an appropriately human way into the void between what we can know, how our desires direct us, and what we are obligated to do. Kant praises "the inscrutable wisdom" as being "not less worthy of veneration in respect for what it denies us than in what it has granted" (V, 148).

This self-insertion is always a synthesis of imagination in which we fashion ourselves as a unique image of freedom. Far from being a counsel of pessimism or a denial of pleasure, the Kantian moral philosophy—from the first to the last—is *ecstatic,* given over to the ever-ongoing creative act of a free being who seeks the best possible life for a human being.

Methodology of Pure Practical Reason

Images and Ecstasy

The Methodology (*Methodenlehre*) of pure theoretical reason concerned itself with "the determinations of the formal conditions of a
complete system of pure reason" (A707–708, B735–36). This determination concerned itself primarily with reason's general task of
holding itself within the limits prescribed by the nature of the elements disclosed in the *Elementarlehre* or, to employ Kant's architectural metaphor of building, instead of "a tower which should reach
to the heavens," "a dwelling-house just sufficient for our business on
the level of experience and just sufficiently high to allow of our overlooking it" (A707, B735). Building and attending to such a dwelling-
house required a great deal of care bestowed upon many different
matters, both concerning the building of the house and the way of
dwelling within it.[1] The Methodology of Pure Practical Reason, by
contrast, is terse. It has only one matter before it, namely "the way
in which we can secure to the laws of pure practical reason *access* to
the human mind and an *influence* on its maxims" (V, 151).

   This section appears to bear at least some external, analogous resemblance to the education of the guardians in Plato's *Republic*. As in
the latter, the image-making machinery is directed toward the human soul in order to shape its responses in a certain way. The differences, of course, are clear. The image-education of the guardians is

designed to produce warriors who will identify their own good with what is good for their city. Further, the guardians are lied to at every turn.[2] But the similarity rests upon their common goal of directing desire away from natural "sensuous attachments" (in Kant's language) to a moral steadfastness analogous to the steadfastness of the Platonic guardian in the face of danger.

Despite this analogical similarity, a similarity that would reinforce the traditional view of Kant's moral philosophy as austere and ascetic, I suggest that the practical *Methodenlehre* makes the case clearly and positively for the view that has been suggested throughout this interpretation but could only come forth properly now. Not only is it mistaken to characterize Kant's moral philosophy in such gray terms, but it misses its fundamental truth: this is an *ecstatic* view of human beings, presenting a possibility of life heretofore unsuspected (although, in my view, present also in the playfulness of the Platonic dialogues, which the Kantian critiques resemble both so little and so much). The selection of images, as will soon be shown, is designed to provide access to that ecstasy.

By "ecstasy," I intend all of the following meanings simultaneously: (1) in its literal Greek sense of *ek-stasis*, standing outside, here outside the pathological, time-determined order of sensation, but also (2) for Kant, given our finitude, ecstasy means standing at once outside/inside this order, i.e., capable of an originary self-insertion into the order of sensation, from a heterogeneous, intelligible source, and finally (3) in its more common English meaning as rapture, thrill, elation.

The general task is "to bring either an as yet uneducated or a depraved (*verwildestes*) mind onto the track of the morally good" (V, 152). This requires an initial address to the causally determined side of our nature through external appeals to advantage or harm, followed by appeals to "the pure moral motive." By this means, "in teaching a man to feel his own worth, it gives his mind a power, unexpected even by himself, to pull himself loose from all sensuous attachments (so far as they would govern him) and, in the independence of his intelligible nature and in the greatness of soul to which he sees himself called (*bestimmt sieht*), to find himself richly compensated for the sacrifice he makes" (V, 152). Kant notes that this method has never been widely used, so its results in experience cannot be assessed. However, the receptivity of human beings to such a method can be adduced.

This first exposition gives a glimpse of the ecstatic nature of morality for Kant. In the very act of conceiving the pure moral motive as a living possibility, the measure of life is transformed for the human being in such a way that the manifest pleasures of sensuous existence are *experienced* as small by comparison. Such a qualitative leap is accomplished, once again, by self-effacing imagination extending the possibility of the human across a gap that would otherwise be unbridgeable, producing a result—here, the consciousness of a self-determining value beyond all price—in excess of the materials at hand, yet utterly decisive.

The outline Kant gives of the methodology of pure practical reason suggests that this methodology involves a *purification process* that is clearly delineated and accessible to all. This distinguishes it from the analogous process in the *Critique of Pure Reason* that involved many technical matters accessible only to people thoroughly trained in academic philosophy (however important these matters are to the securing of "universal human happiness, the principal purpose" [A851, B879]).[3] This process can be discerned in everyday human conversation concerning the moral worth of particular actions, where participants are eager to assess motives of others according to the strictest moral standards.

Kant's "methodology" seems to consist in little more than refining this process by referring such reflections to the standard imposed by the purity of motives enjoined by the moral law. He recommends "biographies of ancient and modern times" to the educators of young people, since these abound with examples of actions of all kinds that could be used as springs for the cultivation of youthful moral judgment through directed discussion. Similarly, examples from history and literature can be used to impress upon young minds the wondrousness of acting from pure motives that hold themselves apart from all sensuous reward and punishment.[4] As Socrates tells Theaetetus in the dialogue bearing the latter's name, the love of wisdom begins in wonder (155d2–5).

One can see this methodology as a gradual redirection of the imagination away from actual images to the pure, ruling image in terms of which the human being can enact her or his unique human life, or "unique phenomenon." This cultivation involves a redirection of moral reflection from inspection of the (supposed) motives of others to inspection of one's own motives. It also serves as preparation for the self-examination spoken of above in the comments to the "Critical Elucidation of the Analytic of Pure Practical Reason," for the sake of the quality of one's life in the future.

This quality can clearly be described as "ecstasy" in the first sense noted above, namely as outside the series of phenomenal conditions. One can also discern the second sense, insofar as one finds oneself located within these conditions even as one is shown another measure. The case for the third sense, ecstasy as rapture, seems difficult if not impossible to make, especially in the face of such Kantian comments as "it is in suffering that [the law of morals and the image of holiness and virtue] most notably show themselves"[5] (V, 156). However, this self-showing is only a prelude to the way this law and those images gain access to the human mind. By making them manifest in their purity, they can be beheld in their wondrousness. By their means alone, one can strengthen and elevate oneself into a realm of freedom beyond the pull of mere sensation.

In this light, one cannot merely prefer the image of a suffering Thomas More to the greatest riches or most sybaritic pleasures. Instructed by such images to one's own moral capacity, one can much more importantly enact moral principles in one's own unique life. Principles based upon concepts must guide, Kant says, but "we must see the representation (*Vorstellung*) of them in relation to the human being and to his individuality (*Individuum*); for then the law appears in a form (*Gestalt*) which is indeed deserving of highest respect" (V, 157–58). Such a representation compels the renunciation of sensuous inclination as the determining motive of human action. Thus, this *moral* compulsion occurs *against* its competing compulsion, the compulsion of *natural* inclination.

Moral compulsion, then, compels in a peculiar way. It holds up an image of humanity that counters the latter compulsion such as to reduce its influence, but does so in a way that allows *voluntary* assent or denial! This is Kant's remarkable conception of the human: a being given over to *voluntary compulsion*. If one chooses the moral life, one renounces the pleasures of sense and the happiness attending to their satisfaction. The trade-off: self-respect, and the elevation and inner strength that flow from it. But this trade-off requires constant vigilance, because the incentives of (sensuous) happiness never cease, and because one's own motives—even after making this choice—are always subject to critique. Nevertheless, the access provided by the Methodology of Pure Practical Reason is at once access to its object, the highest good. In the highest good one finds a happiness suitable to a human being—a being who must erect a dwelling in proportion to the elements at her or his disposal.

Interestingly, Kant proposes that the ultimate result of this cultivated feeling of the extension of our powers beyond the pull of sensation is first a "liking (*lieb*)" (V, 160), secondly "satisfaction (*Zufriedenheit*)" together with the "lifting of a burden" (both V, 161). Between these two outcomes from the two express steps of the methodology[6] lies a bridge, namely "this occupation of the faculty of judgment (*Urteilskraft*)" in which the understanding and imagination find themselves in harmony. This mediating function "is not yet interest in actions and their morality itself" (all V, 160).

The ascending progress is presented as habit → disinterested judgment (harmony of understanding and imagination and the resulting disinterested pleasure) → morality, or in other words "liking" → beauty[7] → contentment. This ascent also has a humorous side: Kant presents Leibniz's coming to "like" and then to release an insect from which he derived much instruction, accordingly much disinterested pleasure, and a consequent feeling of self-sufficiency.

To be sure, human self-sufficiency is limited. We remain, like Leibniz's favored insect (and like Leibniz!), beings of need. Our being enough (*genug*) for ourselves implies only that we have the means of ascent suitable to our limited nature. We can determine to live out our own lives in accord with the moral law so that these lives are unique images of freedom. Our contentment images that happiness in accord with our nature, not the kind of happiness associated with luxury and indulgence decried by Socrates in Book IV of the *Republic*

(419A–420A). Yet can it not, *must* it not be said that the strength, resolve, and elevation that derives from giving oneself over freely to the moral law necessarily produces rapture, thrill taken in the simple existential truth that one is a human being living out one's humanity in the best possible way?

After all, contentment for a human being in Kant's thought cannot possibly refer to untroubled tranquility. Rather, it must refer to the gratification taken in the power to wage an ever-ongoing struggle successfully amidst a most enticing play of images. The moral life is at once voluntary surrender to the command of the moral law, and triumphant victory over the incentives that would derail one from one's own unique best life. It is ecstasy.

Conclusion(s)

To Kant's Text

The "ever new and increasing admiration and awe" (V, 161) provoked by the starry heavens and the moral law require philosophy for direction. Without them, the former becomes the subject for astrology, the latter for fanaticism and superstition. Both require philosophy in order for that primordial wonder to be properly channeled. More precisely, "science (critically sought and methodically directed) is the narrow gate that leads to the *doctrine of wisdom*" (V, 163, emphasis in original), and philosophy is the guardian of that science.

But as Kant has already written in the *Methodenlehre* of the *Critique of Pure Reason*, "Indeed it is precisely in knowing its limits that philosophy consists" (A727, B755). As I have endeavored to show throughout, Kantian philosophy consists of the limiting of theoretical knowledge to the sensible realm by means of the schemata, and the limiting of moral insight to the imaginative positing of an intelligible realm governed by the moral law. The former surely limits the study of the stars and the elements to astronomy, chemistry, and physics respectively. The latter just as surely limits moral maxims to those that can be universalized. Both, however, issue from the power of imagination to synthesize concepts (and, in the case of theoretical reason, pure intuition as well) into principles and, from this same power, to produce ruling images by means of which human experience has sense and significance. The "doctrine of wisdom," then, includes a concealed paean to imagination.

To This Interpretation:

The exegetical task of determining the role of imagination in the *Critique of Practical Reason* seemed daunting if not impossible at its outset, given Kant's apparent exclusion of imagination from moral reasoning. In reading the text closely, however, imagination showed itself to have both a prominent and a central role. As Kant noted at A78, B104 of the *Critique of Pure Reason* where it is declared to be the source of synthesis in general, imagination is both blind and indispensable, and we are scarcely ever conscious of it. As I have tried to show throughout, imagination is most fully present precisely where it is most completely concealed.

Imagination is the source of synthesis. The moral law is a synthetic *a priori* judgment. Therefore imagination must be at work in effecting this synthesis. Maxims fashioned in accord with the moral law are likewise synthetic and so involve imagination. Applying these maxims *in concreto*, since this involves crossing from one realm (the intelligible) to another that is different in kind (the sensible), also involves synthesis and thus also involves imagination.

Imagination also produces images. The moral law is itself a pure image, not itself a law but the pure form of a law in general. When one thinks it, one has this pure image in view. The highest good, the object of a will that would act from the moral law in which happiness is granted in proportion to moral worth, is also a pure image. It is that pure vicarious image toward which the human being directs herself or himself, so that the natural inclination toward happiness finds its appropriate outlet.

The moral self-examination one can make of one's past maxims, which might be called the Delphic counterpart in Kant, results in a human life interpreted as a unique phenomenon. Every element of this self-examination has imagination's trace upon it: the moral law itself, the holding of the maxims (moral or not) that one has employed throughout one's phenomenal life, the application of these maxims to the actions recalled, the life recollected as unique phenomenon, and the future life one projects as the completion of the unique phenomenon under the instruction of this self-examination.

Further, the interpretation of one's own life as unique self-determined phenomenon exceeds the architectonic structure Kant has provided for its discernment, as discussed in the discussion of the Critical Elucidation of the Analytic above. Neither a pure product of the intellect like the moral law nor like an empirical occurrence according to the natural law of causality, a human life subjected to (and then guided by) such self-examination must be seen as a work of art—again, a product of imagination.

The *Methodenlehre* seems to be devoted entirely to the manipulation of images by reason in service to the cultivation of the moral life. However, the selection of images for the sake of stimulating the moral incentive must be made across the gap of intelligible and sensible and so involves imagination. And the elements, once again, require synthesis for their very conception. Finally, the *Methodenlehre* discloses an image of the moral life as an ecstatic life, a life in comparison with which the satisfaction of pathological desires is worth little or nothing.

Before ending this section, it may be useful to revisit the question of why Kant, on several occasions in the *Critique of Practical Reason*, chose to exclude or to denigrate imagination's role in key sections of the *Critique of Practical Reason*. In the Typic of Pure Practical Judgment, for example, where one would expect at least a nod in its direction, Kant insisted that "understanding (and not the imagination)" (V, 69) is the faculty at work in mediating the application of the moral law to nature. And in the section on the Primacy of Pure Practical Reason, Kant delineates the role of practical reason in holding theoretical reason so that it is not "opening itself to every nonsense or delusion (*Unsinn oder Wahnsinn*) of the imagination" (V, 121).

In the Prologue, I suggested that the Heideggerian claim of a recoil (*Zurückweichen*) by Kant from the insight that would locate imagination as the common root of sensibility and understanding could be resolved less radically. However, there is no doubt that

Heidegger, and later Sallis, cleared the path for this resolution. Resources within the text itself of the *Critique of Pure Reason* provide a clear line of argumentation supporting the primacy of imagination, if one saw imagination in creative tension with the other elements. This is why I claimed and claim that what may have seemed like a radical reading of the first critique by Heidegger was, according to the strictest and most traditional scholarly standards, the correct one.

What can be said in this regard concerning the *Critique of Practical Reason*, where no textual prominence is afforded imagination at all? I claim that Kant indeed drew back, as Heidegger suggested, but for less dramatic reasons. From his experience with the widespread misunderstanding of the *Critique of Pure Reason* by so many of his learned contemporaries, Kant wrote more simply. The B Deduction, for example, in which imagination does not occur until quite late but plays the decisive role, is structured in a way that is far easier to follow than the A Deduction, where imagination is present at the outset and throughout.[1] The B edition made Kant less likely to be mistaken for a Berkleyan, as Garve and Feder did in their influential review, but §24 re-establishes its centrality.

In this light, one can only wonder in distress what would be made of a moral philosophy in which imagination was included as an essential component, even though the Kantian imagination is as far as possible from being merely a source of *Unsinn und Wahnsinn*. As Kant noted in a key passage of the section on the Primacy of Pure Practical Reason also cited above, "it is one and the same reason which judges *a priori* by principles, whether for theoretical or for practical purposes" (V, 121). Judgment *must* involve synthesis if it is to effect either morality or experience of nature, so it *must* involve imagination; the Kantian philosophy requires this conclusion. Despite imagination's absence in the printed words of the text, imagination is fully present *in* and *throughout* the *Critique of Practical Reason*.

Imagination and Depth

An account of depth is especially called for in our current philosophical climate, where the anti-foundationalism dominating both sides of the philosophical divide obscures this crucial part of our experience and lets it slip out of view. By depth, I mean nothing abstruse. Everyday objects, works of art, intentional objects, etc. are *deep* in the sense that they at least seem to point beyond themselves. However, philosophical accounting for the phenomenon of depth required and requires much more.

Kant's thought provides an especially good site at which to engage this phenomenon. This is so because the critical philosophy of Kant shares a common interest with both sides of our divide. Despite its temporal distance from and marked difference in form from today's philosophical forays, I believe that this distance and this difference can aid us in recovering a rich philosophical sense of depth.

The commonness with Kant to which I refer is an abiding concern on both sides with language, its nature and its limits. The difference is both striking and challenging. Language could never be regarded by Kant either as a function of formal logic or as a semantic/syntactic system that has been somehow compromised in advance. Language for Kant was always *judgment*, in particular synthetic *a priori* judgment. The simplest tautology or observation of the world of sense required the formidable apparatus of pure reason, with imagination as synthesizer/producer of images at the center. That is to say, even the barest pronouncement pointed beyond itself to a concealed depth that made it possible.[2]

As discussed in the first chapter, freedom has no antecedent, is the product of no inference and is governed by no principle. It is spontaneous and intelligible, but given the generally uncreative nature of reason, there is only one way to account for Kant's claim that reason has created this concept. Reason, regarded as the entire higher faculty, includes *imagination* as its only creative element. Freedom is the pure product of imagination, extending itself into the gap of our causal knowledge out of nowhere. Its "law," the moral law, is a law only in an ambiguous sense: it is the pure form of a law in general.

In this sense, one can see rather easily how imagination functions as the concealed depth of human action, although this depth lies in a greater darkness than the depth belonging to the sciences. Human actions are one and all phenomenal, and so subject to the causality of nature. However, at the same time we must presuppose them as the product of freedom, of freely chosen maxims. Like the laws of science, one can infer them from the appearances and even test them. A person can determine, for example, whether another person is generally trustworthy or not, and so infer the person's maxim of action. However, unlike the laws of physics, for example, the maxims of a person's actions (including and perhaps especially one's own) cannot be said to be *known* at all. They can merely be said to follow from the actions to the presupposition of spontaneous, intelligible freedom.

Further, as Kant reminds us often, the question as to the source of our freedom—the answer to the question of why we are free—has no answer. All we can comprehend of the moral law, to which we are in any case bound, is its ultimate incomprehensibility. This incomprehensibility extends downward to theoretical reason as well. Why we have just a certain set of categories and no other, why we have just this form of intuition and no other—these matters are entirely dark to us. But these categories and that intuition can, by means of the schemata, form principles that can yield knowledge of objects of experience. We can avail ourselves of no such knowledge in the practical realm.

However, only in the practical realm can I liberate myself from the otherwise unavoidable entanglements and illusions that obtain when reason seeks to overstep the sensible condition to which I am bound. Without freedom as the keystone, I may commit the *hubris* of concluding to the absolute duration of my soul (paralogisms). I may also mistakenly conclude to the existence of a God that would render my actions subject to external determination and so deprive them of any possible worth. And by abandoning freedom to a competition with natural necessity that it cannot win but can only remain in perpetual strife, I would call all human action into question regarding its moral meaningfulness.

In other words, by searching for theoretical knowledge without justification in the realm of the supersensible, the failure of this search is guaranteed. Only by practical reason's closing off that realm from theoretical knowledge by *asserting* the reality of freedom without actually knowing it can theoretical reason accomplish its work at all, and can the ideas of immortality and God find their proper place within the play of the human condition.

Finally, only imagination, as the hidden depth of this positing of freedom and of all that is connected with it, fashions the edifice of the system of reason, just as it fashions the edifice we humans build in our souls for ourselves.

From the *Critique of Practical Reason* to the *Critique of Judgment*

Both in its Dialectic and in its Methodology, the *Critique of Pure Reason* provided a clear textual path to the *Critique of Practical Reason*. In the Dialectic, the early "denial of knowledge to make room for belief" was no mere personal renunciation and affirmation. Rather, it was shown to have its roots in the nature and limits of reason itself. Further, the ever-present but more obscure and deeper path through the *Critique of Pure Reason*, the path of synthesis-producing and image-making imagination, showed itself to also be of first importance in this transition. Section 3 of the Discipline of Pure Reason, as treated in the Introduction above, ascribes an expressly creative power to imagination, an ascription that at least nears an affirmation of imagination's power (under the guidance of reason) to bring the practical realm itself into being (A769–70, B797–98).

The Third Antinomy proved the logical possibility of the idea of freedom, keystone (*Schlußstein*) not only of the *Critique of Practical Reason* but also of reason's whole systematic edifice. The Canon of Pure Reason concluded with the (somewhat playfully) apologetic claim that the sole achievement of pure reason in opening up prospects beyond the realm of experience consists of two articles of belief, the immortality of the soul and the existence of God. Imagination generated both the extension of the category of causality such that the Third Antinomy arose and ultimately showed that free will and natural necessity were not contradictory to one another, i.e., that they could a least be *thought* together. Also, the extensions of the categories of substance and community to the ideas of the soul (immortality) and God (existence) proved thinkable, though it remained for the *Critique of Practical Reason* to exhibit the proper place of these elements in the systematic edifice of reason, namely as postulates of pure practical reason.

The *Critique of Practical Reason* seemed to provide an insurmountable obstacle to the disclosure of the ever-present but more obscure and deeper path of imagination, if such a path existed at all. Kant himself appeared to have denied imagination such a role. However, I pay myself the compliment of not only having overcome this mistaken view, but also of having exposed the pre-eminence of imagination as the driver of practical reason. I believe the interpretation offered in this book is entirely faithful to Kant's doctrine of *synthesis*, which is the engine of all three critiques.

However, the *Critique of Practical Reason* does not provide a transition to the *Critique of Judgment* that is nearly as smooth either textually or substantively as the one from the *Critique of Pure Reason* to the practical critique. There are, to be sure, *some* indications. Leibniz's favored insect (V, 160, 285), discussed above, provides one. The brief description of imagination (V, 160), also discussed above, provides another. But nothing in the second critique comes close to providing the extensiveness and richness of argumentation or the far-reaching philosophizing that would allow for an authoritative transition to the third. Those scholars who see the *Critique of Judgment* as almost an afterthought to the first two critiques would seem to have some evidence on their side.

Kant's December 1787 letter to Reinhold, after he has completed the *Critique of Practical Reason* but before its actual publication, appears to lend at least some support to this view. The following is excerpted from that letter:

> My inner conviction grows, as I discover in working on different topics, that not only does my system remain self-consistent but also, when

sometimes I cannot see the right way to investigate a certain subject, I find that I need only look back at the general picture of the elements of knowledge, and of the mental powers pertaining to them, in order to discover elucidations that I had not expected. I am now at work on a critique of taste, and I have discovered a kind of *a priori* principle different from those heretofore observed. For there are three faculties of the mind: the faculty of cognition, the faculty of feeling pleasure and displeasure, and the faculty of desire. In the *Critique of Pure* (theoretical) *Reason*, I found *a priori* principles for the first of these, and in the *Critique of Practical Reason* I found *a priori* principles for the third. I tried to find them for the second as well, and though I thought it impossible to find such principles, the systematic nature of the analysis of the previously mentioned faculties of the human mind allowed me to discover them.[1]

In the main part of this text, I explicitly excluded consideration of imagination in the *Critique of Judgment* as an aid of any kind in the explication of imagination's role in the second critique. The principal goal of this book has been to let imagination show itself even and especially where it seems to be entirely absent, and to do so in terms internal to the work. To exploit the apparently much more liberal employment of imagination in the third critique would only defeat that purpose. However, as will soon become apparent, I am now in position to give a reason that *is* deeper and more internal to the Kantian problematic.

In reading the 1787 letter to Reinhold, then surveying the first two critiques, it does not seem difficult (at least retrospectively) to discern that *purpose* plays a major role in both. First of all, the three faculties of the mind were already acknowledged in the *Critique of Pure Reason*. By excluding "the will and the feeling of pleasure and pain" (A49, B66) from the theoretical critique, Kant tacitly affirms them as mental components. They become, of course, the subject matters of the *Critique of Practical Reason* and the *Critique of Judgment* respectively. The 1787 letter merely gestures at the difficulty of locating *a priori* principles for the feeling of pleasure and pain.

In the first critique, Kant declares purposive unity to be the highest unity of all. It consciously or unconsciously drives our search for completeness under one highest principle in all of our theoretical investigations. In the second critique, the highest good is the ultimate purpose of humanity, and the ultimate purpose of creation is moral purpose. Thus "purpose" in some sense, a sense later developed in the *Critique of Judgment* as *purposiveness* (*Zweckmässigkeit*), serves as the "missing" *a priori* ground of the third faculty of the mind, arrived at by the almost embarrassingly modest expedient of a disjunctive syllogism that had somehow been overlooked for years.

It then only remains for the astute commentator to read the Introduction to the *Critique of Judgment* and follow Kant's chart at its end to reach the conclusion that the notion of purposiveness is a product of imagination. Purposiveness bridges the sensible realm as determined in the first critique with the supersensible realm determined in the second, and so brings them to unity. At least by analogy if not by originary synthesis, imagination serves as the "between" or even the "original" whereby understanding (as provider of the laws governing sensation) and reason (as provider of the laws governing morality) are harmonized. Kant appears to endorse this view when he says there is the feeling of pleasure "between the faculties of knowledge and desire." It might seem to follow *a fortiori* that the principle governing the feeling of pleasure and pain can also be placed quite straightforwardly between the principles of the other two faculties of the mind.

If only matters were so direct and simple! The difficulty, easy to notice but just as easy either to forget or make light of, resides in the distinctive nature of *judgment* (*Urteilskraft*) in the third critique. Although Kant took great pains to delineate this distinctiveness and sustain it throughout both his first introduction which he did not publish[2] and in the actual Introduction, astute readers of Kant have often confounded them, somehow finding material in the *Critique of Judgment* that they claim undermines or overcomes major claims in the *Critique of Pure Reason*.[3]

The principal discovery that made the "critique of taste" possible is the detection of *reflective judgment,* a way of judgment that differs in *kind* from and begets judgments other than what Kant calls the *determinative* judgments of the *Critique of Pure Reason*. This mere textual point alone is enough, in my view, to establish the inappropriateness of employing the *Critique of Judgment* as some kind of key to unlocking, or perhaps "loosening up," the supposed austerity prescribed by the *Critique of Practical Reason*.

Kant characterizes the distinction between the two kinds of judgment as follows: "If the universal (the rule, the principle, the law) is given, that subsumes the particular . . . the judgment is *determinative*. But if only the particular is given [as the basis] from which the universal is to be found, the judgment is **merely** *reflective*" (V, 179, emphases on "determinative" and "reflective" in original, bolding of "merely" mine). Accordingly, determinative judgments concern themselves with objectively necessary laws and the way these laws make their realms possible. They possess both objective and subjective validity. Reflective judgments, on the other hand, are only subjectively valid. That is the reason for Kant's modifier "merely" above, and for my emphasis on it.

Reflective judgments have nothing whatsoever to contribute either to moral or to theoretical knowledge. Like so much else in the critical philosophy, the depth that gives rise to this surface requires close attention both to Kantian principles and claims and to the way the latter reflect back upon his own texts when they are closely examined.

What internal and perhaps deeply concealed material in the *Critique of Practical Reason* suggests itself as providing a transition to the *Critique of Judgment*? First and foremost, the *ecstasy* belonging to self-elevation is particularly well-suited to disclose a pure region of pleasure and pain. Each fold of the threefold meanings of ecstasy serves this disclosure: a dwelling *outside* (the literal Greek sense of *ek-stasis*) the pathological realm of sensation, a capability of an originary self-insertion of the moral law *into* the latter realm, and primordial elation as taking pleasure in the dignity of one's own humanity.

It is called a Methodology of *Pure* Practical Reason because its task is the elevation of the heretofore uneducated or savage (*verwildestes*) mind. But it is time to ask: From what source does the speech in the Methodology arise? Further, who is being addressed in this section? In a superficial sense, a morally mature teacher provides appropriate images ("biographies of ancient and modern times") to stimulate moral reflection and encourage its ongoing practice. In a deeper sense, however, it is not Kant or any morally mature teacher speaking, but *pure practical reason itself*.

Given our nature as beings of need and the consequent impossibility of our acting entirely from moral motives, we humans are all in some sense uneducated and perhaps even savage as well. Thus we humans require *images* of a certain kind to elevate us from pathological to moral principles. The standard for the appropriateness of these images is determined not by any particular person or teacher, but by pure practical reason. The educational role and how well it is performed is measured by the way any teacher (or any student!) interprets the images under the sway of the moral law.

Here, then, reflective judgment begins to show itself both between the folds of the sensible and supersensible realm, as their support, and as the *a priori* possibility of the subjective transition. Suppose I, with Kant's *Critique of Practical Reason* as my guide, were to masquerade as a "mature moral teacher." Accordingly, I choose to seek biographies as sources of instruction. How would I go about selecting an appropriate biography? How can I conduct and/or participate in discussions focusing upon the moral behavior of the characters appearing in the biographies, being morally imperfect myself?

It is clear that I do neither without there being some prior grasp of the principles underlying the breach between sensible and supersensible, i.e., without my already having the capacity to compare the objective principles governing human actions with the salient details of the lives. Kant's example of Thomas More is surely worthy studying, and it provides a model capable of elevating almost anyone's soul. But what about powerful but morally more complex personages, such as Caius Marcius Coriolanus in Plutarch's biography? Certainly qualities that may be deemed morally admirable in some respects— such as loyalty to family, loyalty to country, love of honor, courage, and even a certain innocence—can be shown by means of reflective discussion to have their limits. Simultaneously, the manipulative evil of the tribunes and the gentle wisdom of Menenius Agrippa can provide counterpoint, as they can raise the question (and disjunction!) of social position in relation to morality.

Epilogue

The selection of a *particular* biography that will serve to enable the discovery of the universal moral law clearly requires a reflective judgment and not a determinative one. This is so whether the biography discloses the universal directly, as in the biography of Thomas More, or indirectly, as in the biography of Caius Marcius. So, too, does the discussion. As Kant notes, such biographies can awaken and can strengthen a moral sense in the young—but not only in the young. In both the selection and the discussion, imagination has already synthesized the moral and sensible realms in a certain way, and has already provided the support and the measure for any educational venture.

But it is of the highest importance to remember that this synthesis is an *entirely subjective* synthesis. It is of similar importance to note that if one is called upon to characterize the epistemological status of this synthesis, it would have to be called a *pure image*. Most emphatically, there is no claim that the two realms *really are* brought together, but only that imagination brings them together *in the subject*. This insight has major philosophical consequences.

First, as the *Critique of Judgment* will show in §59, the transition from pleasure in sensation to respect for the morally good is only *indirect* and ultimately *analogical*. *The pure image can determine nothing whatsoever.* It must be seen only as *offering a bond* between the two realms. The pure image, at its very most powerful, is a solicitation to that transition given by every human subject to itself as a possibility.

Second, imagination's subjective fashioning of a pure image always already uniting sensible and supersensible sheds further light on the nature of the human subject. The Paralogisms of the *Critique of Pure Reason* demonstrated that the human subject was divided from itself: the "I" that thinks through the categories (the "substantial" I) and the "I" that is thought through the categories (the "I" as inner sense, as appearance) are not the same. The *Critique of Practical Reason* demonstrated the division of the "I" from itself in another way. The intelligible "I" who can posit the moral law that commands absolutely must struggle with the "I" as a pathologically determined being, so that the former "I" may freely act under the moral law and in its spirit.

Third, in the reflective judgment's subjective pure image, which bridges both theoretical and practical realms, the necessarily fractured, self-alienated subject finds itself in a certain kind of harmony with itself. Quite remarkably, this harmony cannot occur in either the realm of sense or in the realm of morals. Self-alienation necessarily belongs to both realms. Looked at in terms of Kantian logic, the determinative judgment guarantees that the subject must deal in an ongoing fashion with material that is recalcitrant by its very nature. Theoretical reason must, in its research, at once always deal only with the heterogeneously given sensuous manifold as it must also remain watchful of reason's propensity to transgress its limits. Practical reason must both overcome the charms of sense, the pull of self-love, and the ambiguity of its own motives even when the moral law is invoked. The freedom belonging to practical reason (and *a fortiori* to theoretical reason) is autonomy, self-*rule*. Only the freedom belonging to reflective judgment is freedom without the compulsion of a rule.

How does Kant characterize this freedom in the early stages of the *Critique of Judgment*, and precisely how does it differ from autonomy? In the Introduction, Kant makes the following distinction:

> The judgment has therefore also . . . in itself a principle *a priori* of the possibility of nature, but only in a subjective aspect, by which it prescribes not to nature (autonomy), but to itself (heautonomy) a law for its reflection upon nature. (V, 185–86)

This law holds for all investigation of nature insofar as such investigation seeks to connect diverse perceptions and to unify them. It also holds for the aesthetic experience of beauty (both natural and artificial). One judges "this rose is beautiful" or "Van Gogh's *Bedroom in Arles* is beautiful," and by virtue of expressing this experience in a singular and therefore universal judgment, one has reflected upon the rose and/or the painting in accord with the aforementioned rule of reflection.

Both judgments presuppose that their objects are already determined as objects. Neither judgment adds a single predicate to these determinate objects, but merely reports the reflective outcome. Along the same lines, "this pastrami sandwich tastes terrific" (in Kantian language " . . . gratifies me") or "I like the pictures of Mickey Mouse at Disney World" cannot be placed in singular judgments in accord with the reflective law.

How does this detachment from the determination of objects affect the freedom peculiar to the third critique? Or, in other words, what constitutes the difference between autonomy and heautonomy? In moral freedom as autonomy, the rule of the self involved a double synthesis of imagination. For one, imagination synthesized the pure elements of maxim formation in general and universal law. For another and simultaneously, imagination applied the individual maxims to nature, including especially human nature, crossing over from the realm of thought to the realm of desire. On one obvious level, moral freedom consisted of the capacity to follow or not to follow the command of the moral law. On a deeper level, it consisted of the lawful play of imagination as it fashioned a world suitable for dignified human dwelling.

The *Critique of Judgment* presupposes the construction of the world of sense by means of the apparatus accounted for in the *Critique of Pure Reason,* in particular imagination as the source of the synthesis/syntheses that have always already occurred. The *Critique of Judgment* also presupposes the constructibility of the moral realm, together with the elements such a structure would have to contain. (One cannot speak of its *actual* construction since the latter requires the free act of the subject.) The possibility of such constructibility rests upon the engagement of imagination in bringing the moral realm into being *for me.*

The full philosophical significance of the opening between natural necessity and freedom first glimpsed in the Third Antinomy makes itself manifest here. The imagination-driven Principles (*Grundsätze*) govern the realm of sensation. No experience of the sensible realm is possible without appearances being magnitudes (both extensive and intensive), without appearances standing in necessary time-relation with one another, and without the judgments concerning these appearances being related to the empirical thought to which human beings are bound by nature. This condition holds for everyone from the most morally wretched to the most morally upright.

The imagination-generated Categorical Imperative governs the moral realm, but unlike its theoretical counterpart, this realm comes into being only for those who freely choose it. The morally wretched among us can enjoy every success that the world of sense has to offer, can also make major contributions in fields important to the welfare of the human race in both science and art, can spread happiness though their naturally cheerful disposition, etc. But in the most important calculus for a human being, none of this matters at all.

Further, it is quite possible that those who choose to govern their lives morally, with the attendant struggles and self-questioning this may entail, may accomplish nothing of note in the world of sensation. Nevertheless, such a life deserves to be celebrated. That imagination belongs to both kinds of choice should go without saying by now. The difference is that there is no creative generation of another unconditional supersensible (moral) realm in the former, but only a realm directed to conditional ends in the realm of sense (love of honor, happiness, reputation, etc.). Considered determinatively, there can be no *direct* transition between the two realms in principle.

The *Critique of Judgment* affirms the possibility of a harmony between sensible and supersensible, but the nature of this harmony is ultimately as dark as its origin. This harmony is purposive, to be sure, but only subjective. It is drawn neither from nature nor from freedom:

> This transcendental concept of a purposiveness of nature is neither a natural concept nor a concept of freedom, because it ascribes nothing to the object (of nature), but only represents the peculiar way in which we must proceed in reflection upon objects of nature in reference to a thoroughly connected experience, and is consequently a subjective principle (maxim) of the judgment. Hence, as if it were a lucky chance favoring our design, and we are rejoiced (*erfreut . . . werden*) properly speaking, relieved of a want if we meet with such systematic unity under merely empirical laws. (V, 184)

The joy taken in the very act of reflectively judging the accidental concurrence of an object of nature foreshadows the disinterested pleasure belonging to the reflective judgment of beauty. This anticipatory afterword is not the place for a systematic discourse on the Analytic of the Beautiful. However, one reference in particular both indicates the harmony, the at-homeness, of the subject with itself and points beyond it to a harmony that is perhaps even more fundamental.

> The subjective universal communicability of the mode of representation in a judgment of taste, since it is to be possible without presupposing a definite concept, can refer to nothing else but the mind in the free play of the understanding and imagination (so far as they agree [*zusammen stimmen*] with one another, which is requisite for cognition in general). (V, 217–18)

First of all, the harmony consists of the unforced, accidental agreement, the "tuning-together," of understanding and imagination. The harmony of self is the reflectively experienced harmony of the faculties of the mind with one another in the presence of the beautiful. Further, the harmony extends outward, at least in principle, much in the manner of Schiller's *An die Freude* calls out to *alle Menschen* to feel the unity of individual, communal, and universal joy.

Third and most provocatively, Kant emphasizes that this "agreement" of the faculties is requisite for "cognition in general," thus of both theoretical and moral cognition. This emphasis may seem to imply that human beings already somehow must stand in the presence of the beautiful in order to think at all. This striking remark is hardly explained, but only illustrated by the general sociability of human beings that is accountable by means of this agreement of the faculties. Not a word is said about the more dramatic implication, which will be treated at the end of this epilogue.

The status of the beautiful in relation to the morally good is the subject of the famous §59, entitled "Of Beauty as the Symbol of the Morally Good." While a schema supplied to an *a priori* concept is a direct presentation (*Darstellung*) or exhibition of that concept, a *symbol* is an indirect presentation. Schematical hypotyposes (presentations, *Darstellungen, exhibitiones*) are called "demonstrative"; the symbolical hypotyposes are called "analogical." Though Kant does not assert this of the former, the schemata require a single function of judgment.[4] Symbolization requires "a double function, first applying the concept to an object of sensible intuition, and then applying a mere rule of reflection made upon that intuition of which the first is only a symbol" (V, 352).

Consider two examples of schematical hypotyposes (i.e., presentations), one mathematical and the other dynamical. "3 mangoes + 2 mangoes = 5 mangoes" presents the *a priori* concept of quantity together with its schema of number. "Penicillin cures many infections" presents the *a priori* concept of causality together with its schema of one intuition following another in time according to a rule. There are several matters worthy of note in these apparently simple examples. First, no notice is taken of the concepts and schemata (i.e., the principles) already operative. The synthesis, the act of imagination that makes the judgment possible, withdraws and must so withdraw.

Like schematization, symbolization simply cannot occur without imagination. An examination of a few of Kant's examples of symbols proves this. First of all, a monarchical state governed by national laws may be represented as a "living body," while such a state ruled by an individual despot may so be represented as a "hand mill" (both V, 352). It is clear that both presentations are symbolical, since there is no direct connection between a monarchy and either of the two presentations.

Kant's other examples seem more manageable. But it is worthy of note that the symbols he chooses are often found in philosophy. "The words *ground* (support, basis) to *depend* (*abhängen*) (to be held up from above), to *flow* from something (instead of, to follow)" (V, 352). "Ground" can be interpreted symbolically as "cause" or as "reason," e.g., "the nutritional data are the ground of my belief that a vegetarian diet promotes health." "*Hängen . . . ab*" can be interpreted as "depends upon the premise," e.g. "Socrates is mortal" depends upon the premise "All men are mortal." "Flows from" can be interpreted as "an effect following a cause," e.g., "Financial security in old age flows from youthful thrift."

In every case, there seems to be little difficulty in grasping the analogy, and just as little in discerning the double function, once the call is made to seek it out. In each case, the specific rule of reflection is an *analogy itself*, understood here as a mere likeness. "Ground" is *like* "reason" in that both suggest support. "Hang from above" is *like* "depend" in that both indicate a prior condition. "Flow from" is *like* "follow" in that both indicate an ordered sequence.

However, this relative ease in following Kant's examples masks a question that goes to the heart of imagination and depth in the *Critique of Judgment* and reflects back upon the transition to it from the *Critique of Practical Reason*. Kant notes, not particularly helpfully, "This matter has not been sufficiently analyzed hitherto, for it deserves a deeper investigation; but this is not the place to linger over (*aufhalten*) it." The question, simply stated, is: how is symbolization possible?

This question is, in its own way, just as important to the Kantian philosophy as the question concerning synthetic judgments *a priori*. In determinative judgments (judgments that involve demonstrative hypotyposes), imagination has always already synthesized pure concepts and pure intuition, and performs empirical syntheses within this always-constituted field. But to all symbolical hypotyposes, which transfer "reflection on an object of intuition to a quite different concept to which perhaps an intuition could never correspond,"[5] a *non-conceptual* synthesis belongs.

Here I risk a preliminary and skeletal "deeper investigation" upon which Kant chose not to linger. There is no determinate conceptual connection between a law-governed or a despotic monarchy on one hand, and a living body or a hand mill on the other. The likeness between them is *an original product of imagination* as it reflects upon each kind of monarchy. That is to say, it is a synthesis that, taking its departure from the concept, produces a likeness by virtue of a *feeling* denoted by the concept or one or more of its predicates. *The "like" is itself the non-conceptual component.*

This explains why, strictly speaking, there can be no *inference* from a symbol to that of which it is the symbol, except in the case of singular judgments. Recalling Kant's initial definition, reflective judgments seek to determine the universal from the particular. Only singular judgments can satisfy this demand, and judgments of beauty are the only singular reflective judgments. The move from beauty to goodness is clearly non-singular, a *bold* move, an invalid inference when considered logically. Therefore, to call beauty the symbol of the morally good is not at all to say that beauty is either a necessary or a sufficient condition for moral goodness. Even the most delicate sensibility in its discernment of beauty need not lead the soul to moral goodness, just as even the coarsest is capable of that same goodness.

Of particular significance here is the third fold of Kant's fourfold analogy between the beautiful and the morally good: "The *freedom* of the imagination (and therefore of the sensibility of our faculty) is represented in judging the beautiful as harmonious with the conformity to law of the understanding (in the moral judgment the freedom of the will is thought as the harmony of the latter with itself, according to universal laws of reason)"[6] (V, 354, emphasis in original).

Analogy, considered in its negative implication, means at least non-identity, non-logical (including non–transcendental-logical) connection. If the relation between beauty and the morally good is analogical, then there is a split between freedom as heautonomy and freedom as autonomy. "Freedom of imagination (and therefore of the sensibility of our faculty)"—what can this mean?

In both the theoretical and practical employments of our reason, the "sensibility of our faculty" was that element that could not be considered as free! In the first case, our (empirical) sensibility is dependent upon an object's being given, and our pure sensibility can only be space and time together with its *a priori* rules. In the second, sensibility was represented as pathological *need*, as far as possible from freedom in any sense.

In both cases, imagination was bound both to conception (understanding) and to intuition (sensibility). In what sense can imagination be free from understanding, and how does this freedom bear upon the remarkable parenthetical remark concerning the consequent freedom of the *sensibility of our faculty*? To the first question, imagination can be free *only in reflection*, but this "only" opens up the possibility of a harmony with oneself elsewhere denied. To the second, "our faculty" refers to imagination itself, which is free to detach itself in reflection from any empirically sensuous content. These two "freedoms" can only be thought together as the non-conceptual reflective synthesis belonging as a possibility to any determinative judgment (synthesis). They are two "freedoms" attaching to the second function of judgment that can be performed by the imagination on any determinative judgment.

Thus "3 mangoes + 2 mangoes = 5 mangoes" produces, on reflection, no universally pleasing conformity between imagination and understanding, nor does "penicillin cures many illnesses," however "good" the latter may be regarded, and however accurate the former. "Van Gogh's *Bedroom in Arles* is beautiful" produces this harmony, insofar at least as the reflective judgment and the experience itself are one. That is, "I see (or imagine) the painting" and "the painting is beautiful" are united. From its epistemologically prior (theoretical) determination of empirical sensibility, imagination reflectively abstracts its image—subtracting both the conceptual and empirical-pathological content—and so bestows upon humanity a gift beyond compare: the possibility of feeling at home with oneself, of feeling entirely in harmony with oneself. This possibility cannot belong to either the theoretical or practical realms, within which striving is made toward some kind of goal that is always beyond our reach.

This is not, of course, the same as *being* at home with oneself. The attainment of full moral virtue would seem required for the latter. Or perhaps more in line with the measure delineated by the *Critique of Practical Reason*, the devotion to the ever-ongoing task of moral improvement, and the effort to liberate oneself from the elements that militate against our dignity and our full humanity, are required. It is obvious that the attainment of full *knowledge* (particularly of the soul, the world, and God) is closed off as a possible home for us, given our bond to appearances and the dialectic that results from ignoring this bond.

To end this epilogue, I return to the question posed earlier, a question raised by what seemed to be an *a fortiori* inference from §9, as drawn above: Given that imagination and understanding must stand in harmony with one another in order for "cognition in general" to occur, must one conclude that human beings must already somehow stand in the beautiful in order to think and to know at all? Once again: "The subjective universal communicability of the mode of representation in a judgment of taste, since it is to be possible without presupposing a definite concept, can refer to nothing else than the state of mind in the free play of the imagination and the understanding (so far as they agree with one another, as is requisite for *cognition in general*) . . . " (V, 217–18, emphasis in original).

The simple answer is "no, human beings do not already somehow stand in the beautiful." Every determinative judgment, whether theoretical or practical, involves a synthesis of *concepts*. All such synthesis calls forth—already has called forth—the alignment of understanding and imagination. This alignment is indeed requisite for cognition, but it has always already taken place without need of the double function. The latter is so because every concept of any kind has a *schema*. On the other hand, the *universal communicability* of the judgment of taste requires that the *free* (i.e., non–concept-governed) play of imagination be in agreement with understanding precisely because *there is no concept* that, with its schema, could align the two. Without this free agreement, no universal communicability of *aesthetic* judgments would be possible.

Thus, it would seem that the feeling at home with oneself afforded by the experience of beauty is surely a wonderful gift, but a rare one. The experience of wonder that occurs in nature from time to time, the delight one takes in a piece of music, a poem, or a painting, for example, are treasured moments—but only fleeting moments when measured against time's succession and against the fear, lust, and death to which human beings are given over. They give us occasions to celebrate the life we are handed, to feel and even to enjoy our humanity fully and freely.

But can this chasm between beauty, theoretical cognition, and practical cognition be the last word? Is there no more than an analogy, then, between beauty, truth, and goodness? Or might there not be a more primordial attunement—perhaps of imagination to itself—concealed in the folds of the *Critique of Judgment* that allows for their more intimate connection?

NOTES

1. I think here especially of Paul Guyer, who treats imagination only fitfully and makes no mention whatsoever of imagination in his general introduction to Kant's thought in a book designed as an overview of the Kantian philosophy. See Paul Guyer, ed., *The Cambridge Companion to Kant* (Cambridge, 1992), 1–25.

2. That is to say, Kant is concerned with establishing the possibility of general metaphysics or rational ontology, and of special metaphysics. The latter consists of three divisions: rational psychology, rational cosmology, and rational theology. Their establishment depends upon the possibility of synthetic judgments *a priori*.

3. The apparently technical word has a less forbidding sound in Greek: Θέσις means "a placing" and σύν means "together."

4. Immanuel Kant, *Critique of Judgment*, trans. J. H. Bernard (New York, 1951).

5. Ibid., p. 206.

6. In addition to calling it the faculty of synthesis, Kant also ascribes clear centrality to imagination at other times: "*the unity of apperception in relation to the synthesis of imagination is the pure understanding*" (A119, emphasis in original). Thus, he declares that the understanding depends upon imagination for its very possibility in the A Deduction. In the B Deduction, he calls imagination "the faculty of representing in intuition an object that is *not itself present*" (B151, emphasis in original). In a striking note, he says "imagination is a necessary ingredient of perception itself" (A120n).

Interestingly, both in the Schematism and in the Ideal, Kant calls the products of imagination *monograms*. In the former, in connection with the categories, they direct the pure synthesis despite their dark origin. In the latter, where reason can provide no such guidance, they form "rather a blurred sketch drawn from diverse experiences than a determinate image—a representation such as painters and physiognomists profess to carry in their heads, and which they treat as being an incommunicable shadowy image of their creations or even of their critical judgments" (A550, B598). At least the former will find greater indulgence in the *Critique of Judgment*.

7. Sallis notes that the metaphorics of tunneling employed by Kant

(A319, B375–76) contains a profound inner tension, namely that the very act of tunneling to bedrock by critique deprives the ground that it would secure of its firmness precisely *by* such tunneling. See Chapter One entitled "Tunnelings": "It is a matter of a fissure within the *Critique of Pure Reason* as a whole, a fissure, a spacing, that makes of it a radically heterogeneous text" (John Sallis, *Spacings—of Reason and Imagination in Texts of Kant, Fichte, Hegel* [Chicago, 1987], 7–8).

8. I borrow this term from Sallis's chapter on Fichte in *Spacings*, 23–66, taking it from that context and employing it here in order to describe a key feature of imagination in the *Critique of Pure Reason* from which Fichte drew so thoroughly.

9. Kant called this table "The Clue (*Leitfaden*) to the Discovery of All Pure Concepts of the Understanding." Therefore, the pure concepts of the understanding are not, strictly speaking, *derived* from the Table of Judgments. As will soon become apparent, the Pure Concepts of the Understanding are epistemologically prior, and the Table of Categories—or any table of merely formal (general, in Kant's word) logic—are parasitical upon and abstracted from the Pure Concepts (Categories). The Table of Judgments can be found on A70, B95. The Table of Categories can be found on A80, B106.

However, in an equally daring interpretation of the Analytic, Beatrice Longuenesse argues, to the contrary, that the Logical Table of Judgments correctly conceived provides what she calls "the guiding thread" that unites the Transcendental Analytic (*Kant and the Capacity to Judge: Sensibility and Discursivity in the Transcendental Analytic*, trans. Charles T. Wolfe [Princeton, 2002]). While this interpretation seems, on its surface, diametrically opposed to mine, I find a deep inner kinship. Quite remarkably, she also claims that "on several points, my analysis is closer to [Heidegger's] than any other I am acquainted with. . . . Where I disagree with Heidegger is his explanation of the 'same function . . . ,'" which Heidegger famously ascribes to imagination as the common root and as having always already accomplished its synthesis. Longuenesse, by contrast, insists that imagination produces the unity of synthesis "*only if* it is *under the unity of apperception,* which is "the *Vermögen zu Urteile* whose specifications make up the table of judgment" (203–204, emphasis in original).

I am quite willing to grant Longuenesse's distinction in function between imagination and apperception (and thus take a small distance from Heidegger's view), but I deny the progressive development beginning from logical function through deduction and schematism to principles that she favors. This is a real and substantive difference. Nevertheless, in my opinion her book deserves the very highest respect for its fidelity, thoroughness, and originality.

Might one hope for the day when the equally and wrongly discredited Table of Judgments and Transcendental Synthesis of Imagination properly rise to the center of Kant discussion and scholarship?

10. Given that our experience, to which we are always already given over, involves a time-relation, our ability to discern a law-governed order from a contingent order requires a rule—namely the category of cause and effect. We can, however, abstract from this necessary time-order in thought. When we do so, the formal logical relation expressed by hypothetical judgments occurs. These judgments, of course, do not concern objects of experience at all but relationships between truth-values.

The discipline of formal logic has nothing to say about objects of experience, save that contradictions are ruled out—and these are seldom so much as candidates for objects of experience. The law of non-contradiction does, however, have an important role in the Antinomy of Pure Reason. However, "objects of experience" are not at stake there.

11. The term "dogmatic" is descriptive and not pejorative.

12. In Christian Wolff's magnificent title, all of metaphysics is encapsulated —indeed, all of everything!: *Vernünftige Gedanken von Gott, der Welt, der Seele des Menschen auch allen Dingen überhaupt*, 1719 (*Rational Thoughts concerning God, the World, the Human soul, also all Things in general*). I became aware of this title in Lewis White Beck, *Early German Philosophy* (Cambridge, 1969), 257.

The first three parts of the title refer to the three divisions of special metaphysics, the fourth to general metaphysics or ontology.

13. David Hume, *An Enquiry concerning Human Understanding*, in L. A. Selby-Bigge, ed., *Hume's Enquiries, Second Edition* (London, 1963), 75.

14. This "full hearing" must await the Schematism.

15. For a concise, superb account of the importance of imagination and the Schematism, see Hannah Arendt, "Imagination," in Hannah Arendt, *Lectures on Kant's Political Philosophy*, ed. Ronald Beiner (Chicago, 1982), 79–85.

16. The schema of the category of Quantity is *number*, which is made manifest in counting (involving succession). The schema of Quality is the filling of time, which requires measuring quantitative intensity at one (simultaneous) moment.

Since the dynamical categories concern existence of objects (not mere apprehension), their existence for us means existence *in time*. Therefore, each individual category expresses its own time-relation. Accordingly, the schema of substance is permanence of the real in time (i.e., duration); the schema of causality is, as already noted, the real upon which, whenever posited, something else always follows (i.e., succession); the schema of community is the rule-governed coexistence of the determinations of the one substance with those of the other.

As the schema of modality, which presents the relation of judgments to the understanding (and not objects to time and to one another), time itself provides the rule. The schema of Possibility is the determination of the representation of a thing at some time; of Actuality, the schema is existence at some determinate time; of Necessity, the schema is the existence of an object at all times. (See A143, B183–A145, B185 for the source of the lists in this note and its predecessor.)

17. Of the Axioms of Intuition: "All appearances are extensive magnitudes" (B202); of the Anticipations of Perception: "In all appearances, the real that is an object of sensation has intensive magnitude, that is a degree" (B207); of the Analogies of Experience: "Experience is possible only through the representation of a necessary connection of perceptions" (B218). 1. Of the First Analogy: "In all change of appearances substance is permanent" (B224). 2. Of the Second Analogy: "All alterations take place in conformity with the law of the connection of cause and effect" (B232). 3. Of the Third Analogy: "All substances, in so far as they can be perceived to coexist in space, are in thoroughgoing reciprocity" (B256). 4. Of the Postulates of Empirical Thought: 1. Agreement with formal conditions of experience— *possible.* 2. Bound up with material conditions of experience—*actual,* determined in accordance with universal conditions of experience—*necessary.*

INTRODUCTION

1. In *The Gathering of Reason,* Sallis distinguishes four different interpretive strategies: (1) the *duplex,* which most resembles a standard commentary, (2) the *projective,* which is "determined by a subordinate reflection, for example reflecting Kant's concept of reason back into its Greek origin, (3) *inversive,* in which one particular text (the Transcendental Dialectic) is taken as the focal point of the interpretation and other texts are interpreted in its terms so that "a concealed stratum of the focal text can be unearthed," and (4) the *subversive,* which "reinstalls the Kantian texts within the history of metaphysics" in such a way that its various turnings lead the interpretation away from that history and even away from the Kantian texts themselves. The "duplex" interpretation I offer here has substantial overtones of Sallis's other three interpretive modes as well, if indeed a merely duplex interpretation of Kant that explores its depths is even possible. See John Sallis, *The Gathering of Reason* (Athens, 1980), 11–13.

2. Imagination is not mentioned at all in two key essays, both by Guyer, in *The Cambridge Companion to Kant,* which he edited (Cambridge, 1992),

one surveying Kant's intellectual development (1–25) and the other treating the Transcendental Deduction (123–60).

While disagreements between scholars concerning its role and importance in Kant's thought are clearly possible, leaving imagination out of these essays in a volume that purports to be "for new readers and nonspecialists" (back cover) is in my opinion irresponsible, and will surely puzzle those newcomers who find imagination so prominently mentioned. For more on this matter, see my review of *The Cambridge Companion to Kant*. Freydberg, "Anglo-American Kant," *History of European Ideas* (Oxford) 21, no. 1 (1995): 75–80.

3. As mentioned in the Prologue, I will attempt to address aspects of the works of some of its more prominent and more insightful representatives in endnotes. I have tried to find and to note points of convergence and have done so whenever I found them. (In some cases, there were none!) My purpose is to facilitate exchange across the current philosophical divide.

4. These discussions also will take place here in the endnotes.

5. I realize not only is this a provocative claim, given the interpretive stance of this book, but it further marks me—without apology—as one of the few continental writers who is not anti-foundationalist. There are no doubt few on the Anglo-American side as well.

6. While such recourse may be tempting for other reasons, it would bring further problems with it as well, especially with regard to the confounding of determinative judgment and reflective judgment. The dangers of such confounding will be treated in the Epilogue.

7. Here I ask the indulgence of the reader. I prefer translations to be as literal as possible and therefore "Groundwork," as Paton and others have translated it, is preferable to "Foundations" as a rendering of *Grundwerk*. However, the translation from which I will primarily draw (although with changes as seem necessary) is Lewis White Beck's, who is my late and beloved teacher. Immanuel Kant, *Foundations of the Metaphysics of Morals*, trans. Lewis White Beck (Indianapolis and New York, 1978). My main text will therefore say "Foundations," and the translations are rooted in Beck's edition. However, I am ultimately responsible for them all.

All page references to the *Foundations of the Metaphysics of Morals* are drawn from *Kants Werke. Akademie Textausgabe*, Band IV (Berlin, 1968). These references are also included in Beck's translations, at the head of every page.

8. Martin Heidegger, *Kant und das Problem der Metaphysik* (Frankfurt am Main, 1965), 146. Translations mine.

9. Ibid., 147, 149. "Kant ist vor dieser unbekannten Wurzel zurückgewichen" (Kant has recoiled in the face of this unknown root). Heidegger

goes on to say that in the B edition "the transcendental imagination is present only in name."

10. Freydberg, "Concerning 'Syntheses of Understanding' in the B Deduction," in *Proceedings of the Eighth International Kant Congress*, vol. II, pt. I, ed. Hoke Robinson (1995), 287–94.

11. See John Sallis, *Spacings—of Reason and Imagination in Texts of Kant, Fichte, Hegel* (Chicago, 1987), 8–10. There he discusses the tension between the putative "perfect unity" of reason and the various fissures that threaten this unity from within.

12. Since the whole must contain a receptive as well as a spontaneous component, this statement remains quite apt.

13. John Sallis, *The Gathering of Reason*, 157, where he writes "[p]roductive imagination given itself, creates, only the form of its object," and a few sentences later he continues, "Productive imagination *forms* images, brings sense content together in the form of an image."

14. The two sides of the mathematical antinomies can, in these terms, both be dismissed because the pure image of the world generated from the category of causality by imagination can be brought to no *determinate* image whatsoever.

15. "The schema of a pure concept of the understanding can never be brought to any image whatsoever" (A142, B181).

16. Arendt notes, peculiarly in my view, "*Kant's* 'embarrassment in dealing with . . . a power of spontaneously beginning a series of successive things or states'" (B476). See Hannah Arendt, *The Life of the Mind*, vol. 2: *Willing* (New York and London, 1978), 29 (emphasis mine). It is not *Kant's* embarrassment, but rather an "embarrassment" within the thesis position of the Third Antinomy (as she cited correctly earlier, Arendt 20). It is precisely this "embarrassment," challenged by the no less troubled and no less powerful position of the antithesis, that opens up the region of practical reason for Kant.

This is precisely the region to which, in my view, productive imagination extends/has already extended. The darkness surrounding reason's conflict with itself cannot be eradicated, nor can the darkness surrounding the work of imagination. However, the spontaneity of productive imagination "lights up," i.e., exposes the possibility of a good life within the regions accessible to us.

17. Creation in theoretical and practical reason is always undertaken under the guidance of a concept, which provides the limits within which the "creative process" can properly occur. The imagination "creates" the causal field by limiting causes to those events that occur in a necessary time-order. In art, creation occurs without a concept. The gift of the artist "stands in,"

so to speak, for the absent concept. See especially sections §46 and §47 of the *Critique of Judgment*.

18. This is the case so long as the dialectic of reason is critically overcome, and the ideas of reason provide a merely regulative function. If the dialectic remains, i.e., if the ideas are regarded as constitutive, then reason remains at war with itself.

19. Concerning creation in fine art, *genius* serves the creative function. For an account of genius in art, see §§46–50 of the *Critique of Judgment*.

20. Of course, more recent geometries challenge this. But I strongly maintain that this does not alter the fundamental point, namely that the objects of geometry are one and all spatial.

21. This is also its schema of imagination.

22. There, the formulation is slightly different: "I ought never act otherwise than *I could also will that my maxim ought to become a universal law*" (IV, 402).

23. This particular translation departs a great deal from Beck's. Immanuel Kant, *Foundations of the Metaphysics of Morals*, trans. Lewis White Beck (Indianapolis and New York, 1978), 36.

24. Sallis, *The Gathering of Reason*, 176.

25. While Kantian moral philosophy is admired, there is much criticism of its formalism. The work of Ricoeur and Levinas, for example, attempts to shift the ethical focus from respect for humanity based on duty to respect for the Other as Other, the one who has a claim on me and who always effaces and overcomes any distance between us. Ricoeur would remedy Kantian formalism along lines such as the following: "It seems reasonable to approach this difficulty by attempting to place such rational legislation with respect to the *value of the other*. We have said above that it is the other as other and his rights that humble me and fulfill me. In addition, we have spoken of for the other in the same terms as those which Kant uses to describe respect for the law." Paul Ricoeur, *Freedom and Nature: The Voluntary and the Involuntary*, trans. Erazim V. Kohák (Evanston, Ill., 1966), 132.

While he does not mention Kant by name, Levinas takes aim at Kantian ethics in general and its formalism in particular when he writes, "We name this calling into question of my spontaneity by the Other ethics. The strangeness of the Other, his irreducibility to the I, to my thoughts and my possessions, is precisely accomplished as a calling into question of my spontaneity, as ethics." Emmanuel Levinas, *Totality and Infinity*, trans. Alfonso Lingis (Pittsburgh, 1969), 43.

However, Levinas's respect for Kantian ethics is unmistakable: "If one has the right to retain one trait from a philosophical system and neglect all the details of its architecture . . . , we would here think of Kantianism, which finds a meaning to the human without measuring it by ontology and outside the question 'What is there here . . . ?'. . . . The fact that immortality and theology could not determine the categorical imperative signifies the novelty of the Copernican Revolution; a sense that is not measured by being or not being; but being on the contrary is determined on the basis of sense." Emmanuel Levinas, *Otherwise than Being* (Pittsburgh, 1998), 129.

In considering this thoughtful and penetrating approach, I wonder whether the replacement of Kantian formal respect with respect for the ongoing claim of the Other is motivated by the horrendous, monstrous discounting of human life and the utter disregard of individuality in the Nazi Holocaust. According to Kant's formal principle of humanity, there could be no worse outrage than the Holocaust. In that light, I wonder whether the regard for the Other's claim on me can be regarded as an imaginative supplement to Kantian formalism, offered in light of the many horrors of the twentieth century, rather than a replacement.

26. See Sallis, *The Gathering of Reason,* p. 177.

27. Immanuel Kant, *Lectures on Ethics,* trans. Peter Heath (Cambridge, 1997), 139. See also *Kant's Gesammelte Schriften,* Band 27, ed. Royal Prussian (later German) Academy of Sciences (Berlin, 1974), 362.

28. The German word *Imagination* generally refers to reproductive imagination; *Einbildungskraft* to productive imagination. Since these notes were taken by Georg Ludwig Collins during a course given by Kant during the winter semester of 1784–75, it is impossible to be sure what was in Kant's own notes. A non–rule-governed *Einbildungskraft* seems more likely.

29. Kant, *Lectures on Ethics,* 140–41. *Kant's Gesammelte Schriften,* 364.

30. Kant, *Lectures on Ethics,* 141. *Kant's Gesammelte Schriften,* 364–65.

31. The new Cambridge translation fails to follow tradition in sound Kant (and philosophical) translation and so misleads here. Kant's *List* has been traditionally (and far more accurately) rendered as "cunning" by such translators as Gregor. "Wit" is normally reserved for "*Witz*." Heath also translates "idealistic *pleasures*" as "diversions" and "beautiful sciences" (*schöne Wissenschaften*) as "refined forms of Knowledge."

To avoid possible confusion, Mary Gregor's translation of the *Anthropology* treats wit (*Witz*). Kant does not address himself to cunning (*List*) in the *Anthropology.*

32. He calls it a "law" throughout, but most especially on V, 30 where the categorical imperative is called the "fundamental law" (*Grundgesetz*) of Pure Practical Reason. He frequently calls it the "mere form" of a law (e.g., V, 27, 34), also the "mere legislative form of maxims" (V, 28), and "the mere form of giving universal law" (V, 27). This seems to bear out Beck's observation that Kant succeeded in being technical without being precise, but it also bears

out the view—held here—that Kant was delving into uncharted waters that were, are, and will always remain difficult to navigate. As difficult as these distinctions may be to sort through, it does not seem that they make much difference when it comes to human action.

33. An interpretation that moves in a direction entirely different than this one is Samuel J. Kerstein, *Kant's Search for the Supreme Principle of Morality* (Cambridge, 2000). After picking through the arguments and concluding that Kant's derivation of the supreme moral principle "fails utterly," he concludes by saying "a down-to-earth approach to the Kantian project in ethics emerges from this book . . . we need to enter concrete controversies regarding which duties the principle would generate and whether these duties would be acceptable to reflective moral common sense. In searching for the supreme principle of morality, we need to follow the twists and turns of everyday moral experience. There is no royal road to a successful derivation" (187).

Kant's pure apparatus, including perhaps especially productive imagination, surely involves difficulties of negotiation. But what of "reflective moral common sense"? Kerstein clearly wants some other kind of moral measure than Kant's, and some other ethical approach. "Duty" in any acceptable Kantian approach could not be subject to a criterion of "acceptability."

34. The schemata of the pure categories of the understanding bring what I call the *field* of human experience together with its limits into being, doing so without any help or hindrance from us. Transcendental philosophy, Kant says, not only specifies the rules (or, more precisely, the universal condition for rules), but also *a priori* the instances to which the rule is to be applied. For example, while we may indeed be wrong about a particular empirical causal relation, one never mistakes " 'before' and 'after' according to a rule" as the condition for causal connection.

35. "Reality" is a pure concept of the understanding and is incorporated into the second principle of the pure understanding, namely the Anticipations of Perception. This principle reads, "In all appearances, the real that is an object of sensation has intensive magnitude, that is, a degree" (B207). As all our knowledge is bound to sensation, the concept of reality has no other legitimate application. This concept refers to the intensity of the image we are beholding at any moment.

36. The significance of the paralogisms extends far beyond the logical fallacy that they commit. They exhibit a kind of split within the self that cannot be overcome theoretically. In other words, the paralogisms *guarantee* that no theoretical self-knowledge is possible.

In this light, the transition from the theoretical realm to the practical realm, and from theoretical knowing to its practical analogue, takes on special significance. Only in the practical realm does self-knowledge in any genuine sense become possible.

37. The Ideal of Pure Reason serves as the critique for all proofs for the existence of God (A592, B620–A638, B666). Kant arrives at the result that "all merely speculative proofs in the end bring us back to one and the same proof, namely the ontological" (A638, B666).

38. These matters receive much more detailed treatment in the section on the Dialectic of Practical Reason.

I. PRINCIPLES OF PURE PRACTICAL REASON

1. I adopt this way of speaking about the Kantian text based upon conversations with John Sallis years ago. Of course, the sole responsibility for their peculiar use here is mine.

2. As indicated above, the assertion of freedom has its source not merely as a logical need, namely a need for a presupposition in order for moral judgments to have meaning. Such a need clearly could not establish the truth of freedom and of the moral law that is its correlate. Nor does its status as issuing from human finitude establish its being known in the theoretical sense. Practical knowledge, and the principles upon which it rests, are something different entirely. They must be *enacted*, not merely thought, by the human being.

3. "When we come to apply the categorical imperative to *actual* cases—when we have to act or decide—we face the difficulty that, however detailed the subordinate principles previously worked out, however diverse the examples of actions that have been pointed out, these can at most help us discern the moral status of a proposed action, but can never determine fully just what sort of action has been performed" (emphasis mine). Onora O'Neill, *Constructions of Reason: Explorations of Kant's Moral Philosophy* (Cambridge, 1989), 166. She refers the reader to A134, B173 of the *Critique of Pure Reason*, where examples are called "the go-kart of judgment."

I am in complete agreement with O'Neill's interpretation, which admirably notes both the command of the categorical imperative and the difficulties occasioned by that command in decisively determining the moral status of a particular action. I believe that the interpretation offered here strengthens her insight, since imagination's bridging of the heterogeneous divide between intelligible law and sensuous action by its very nature acknowledges the measure of darkness and ignorance to which we are given over, as well as the light that can guide our actions well in the face of this ignorance.

4. Herman offers a view that in an unusual way can be interpreted as cohering with the view offered here on the Kantian passage. Most of the

time, she argues, we do not deliberate morally, but simply act in accord with developed habits (that may themselves have issued from moral deliberation). "Mostly we are to imagine moral judgments being guided by deliberative prescription, and circumstances of conflict come in familiar forms. Moral knowledge accumulates. It is neither reasonable nor necessary to expect a moral theory to do better than this." Barbara Herman, *The Practice of Moral Judgment* (Cambridge, 1993), 158.

Kant's moral theory does much better than this in my view. However, there is concord with Herman's point that appropriate application of a principle to a case grows with increased life experience. Her use of "imagine," while looser than mine, is revealing insofar as "moral judgments," which in this context seem concrete and particular, are spontaneously enacted. Imagination works more ably, although still out of conscious view, in the application of moral principles as experience grows. Further, Kant never suggests that moral acuity does not grow with life experience (nor do I).

5. Allen Wood argues that readers (like myself) are misled when we infer self-opacity from the location of our free agency in an intelligible world, since it would make little sense to limit our empirical self-knowledge in terms of a metaphysical theory the truth of which we can never know. I argue the contrary.

Wood writes, "In fact, Kant's conjectures about noumenal freedom are possible only because we can never have satisfactory empirical knowledge of the mind. If we had reliable access to the natural causes of our behavior, then it would be quite untenable to claim that the real causes are different from these and transcend all experience." See Allen Wood, *Kant's Ethical Thought* (Cambridge, 1999), 201–202.

But the latter conditional, and not only because it is contrary to fact, illuminates nothing. It is not a question of "either-or." The Paralogisms prove beyond a doubt that full self-knowledge—knowledge in which the intelligible and sensible "I" are one and transparent to one another—is impossible. Thus, the self stands in a relationship of some necessary opacity to itself by its very nature.

6. All appearances occur in accord with the principles of theoretical reason. The moral aspect, which arises solely in the intention of the will, is precisely what does not appear.

7. Beck inserts the word "practical" in his translation, though it does not appear in the German text. Nevertheless, this seems to me to be a wise choice given the context and given the possibility that one might devise *some* kinds of laws governed in some way by the desire for happiness.

8. In one of the most acute readings and critiques of Kantian ethics, Lingis fully grasps the reach of what he calls the "moral sense" across the

entire scope of human life. He writes, "The moral sense, the sense of the imperative for law, is for Kant a complex experience, where the subject is simultaneously obedient, imaginative and rigorously cognitive, and where the law is simultaneously an immediate affliction on the understanding and reason, a form imaged in the spectacle of the world, and a project one imposes on oneself." His objection rests upon what he sees as a deeper imperative, one that does not require rational justification. Taking a lovesick Haitian man, who has stopped Lingis's rented Jeep, to Souvenance presents an urgent claim upon him. "To insert a reasoning between that imperative force and my action is only to dally and hold up the urgency of what I have to do." Alfonso Lingis, *The Imperative* (Bloomington, 1998), 196, 220. It seems to me, however, that "a reasoning" has already taken place.

9. Gregor takes an appropriately expansive view of Kant's notion of contradiction in moral matters. "So far as Kant's pre-critical works are concerned, 'to contradict oneself' is to act contrary to the essential ends of humanity, the highest of which is freedom." See Mary Gregor, *Laws of Freedom* (Oxford, 1963), 204.

She also notes how easy it is for critics to take a strictly logical view in order to show that "certain admittedly minimal actions, when universalized, fail to give rise to logical contradiction, while maxims of certain permissible and even obligatory actions contain contradictions." Gregor, 205.

If one is to take a view that is rigorous but not strictly logical, it seems to me that an interpretation in which productive imagination empowers both maxim formation and maxim application provides a positive supplement. My only disagreement with Gregor's view consists of the following, namely that actions never "give rise to" maxims for Kant. Her suggestion regarding the import of the precritical view, however, is rich and useful.

Williams offers a kindred view. He argues that criticisms of Kant's moral "logic" are neither very interesting nor significant, and opts for what he calls an "intuitionist" reading (i.e., one that incorporates "moral seeing") that includes "the doctrine of the spontaneous creative activity of pure practical reason in working on the 'content' of the agent's experience and making known to him through the 'feelings' of 'respect' and 'obligation' how he *ought* to act." See T. C. Williams, *The Concept of the Categorical Imperative* (Oxford, 1968), 134. Again, this view can find ballast within the Kantian text. Recourse to a rule-governed imagination retains the virtues of Williams' criticism of an excessively logical reading of Kant, accounts for its possibility, and strengthens it against charges of arbitrariness.

10. This self-examination bears at least some resemblance, and perhaps a deep one, to the self-examination spoken of by Socrates in Plato's *Phaedrus* 229e–230a. There, Socrates declines to rationalize the myth of Boreas and Oreithyia, for then he would have to do the same for other myths, and for

this he had no time—since another mythical source called him, namely "the Delphic inscription." Where the Socratic self-examination might seem to have a deep affinity with the Kantian one lies in Socrates' wonder whether his destiny is Typhonic or not—in other words, Socrates is inspecting himself for possible transgressions.

11. In the same passage, Kant says, "this consciousness leads directly (*gerade*) to the concept of freedom" (V, 30).

12. Here the consciousness of consciousness can also be included.

13. Plato, *Apology*, 28b–29b.

14. Frank Schalow consciously attempts "an interpretation which allows us to apply Heidegger's analyses from *Being and Time* to redesign Kant's practical philosophy" along existential lines. His project is certainly provocative and well-executed, but I disagree on one quite important matter.

Schalow's analysis of the synthetic power of imagination is superb. In one of many fine passages, he writes, "According to the unique form of projection typical of the imagination, we discover the power to construct for the universality of the rule the image determining the instance of its application." See Frank Schalow, *Imagination: Heidegger's Retrieval of the Kantian Ethic* (Lanham, Md., 1986). However, this sentence immediately follows: "The concrete specification of the case which falls under the rule marks the *a priori* synthesis for practical reason" (169). While I surely agree that imagination projects a pure image, the image can do *no determining*. The pure image and the concrete case are *heterogeneous* in Kant. In my opinion, Schalow has not appropriately accounted for the *self-limiting* function of imagination, though his book certainly emphasizes human finitude.

15. The meaning of "naturally acquired" is different here than in Plato's *Meno*, where it means "by physical birth." Meno understands it to apply to inherited aristocracy, a view that is subjected to withering Socratic *elenchos*.

However, there is a deep affinity here to one aspect of the *Meno*, namely the silence shared by Socrates and Kant on the epistemological status of any claim to virtue.

16. Kant's examples tend to list the duty to preserve one's own life first of all. However, in the *Anthropology* he seems to accord at least relative respect to certain suicides: "it is not always just depraved, worthless souls who decide to rid themselves of the burden of life by suicide; . . . in revolutionary periods, when public injustice is declared lawful (as, for example, under the Committee for Public Safety in the French Republic), honor-loving men (such as Roland) have sought to anticipate by suicide their execution under the law, though under a constitution they themselves would have declared this reprehensible." Immanuel Kant, *Anthropology from a Pragmatic Point of View*, trans. Mary Gregor (The Hague, 1974), 126.

17. In *Republic X*, Socrates notes that "none of the human things is wor-

thy of great seriousness" (604b–c), although he soon concludes with a myth in which the only security for a human being is to attend to what is just.

18. As observed above, particular motives that are species of the desire for happiness yield actions that might be easier to read, but which are either blatantly immoral, or contradictory in comparison, or fail to attain their desired end for many reasons.

19. O'Neill is a particularly astute commentator on this issue. "On Kant's view actual cases of moral deliberation do not use examples at all. When we have to decide what to do we are required to test the principle on which we propose to act according to the Categorical Imperative." Onora O'Neill, *Constructions of Reason: Explorations of Kant's Moral Philosophy* (Cambridge, 1989), 166.

Derrida grasps the radicality of Kant's view: "The example is the only visible of the invisible." After noting the remarkable condition that experience can provide no proof that there is a moral imperative, he writes, "There is no legislator that can be figured outside reason. Put another way, there are only 'figures of the legislator,' never any legislator *proprio sensu.*" In terms of the interpretation here, any "example" (Derrida mentions Moses, Christ, etc.) can function at best as a pure image of reason. See Jacques Derrida, "Passions: 'An Oblique Offering,'" trans. David Wood, in *Derrida: A Critical Reader,* ed. David Wood (Oxford, 1992), 32n10.

20. Kant calls such proofs "apagogical" in the Doctrine of Method of the *Critique of Pure Reason.* While "ostensive" or "direct" proofs are always preferable, since the latter present the grounds upon which the argument is based, apagogical proofs can have more "convincing power" by virtue of their exposure of contradictions (A789–90, B817–18). While no contradiction is exposed here, the *modus tollens* proof effectively exposes the two different measures.

21. This is a parenthetical phrase in the original.

22. For theoretical reason, the objects cause the conceptions that determine the will. For practical reason, the will is the cause of the objects.

23. Korsgaard claims that, with respect to lying, Kant has a "double-level theory." See Christine Korsgaard, *Creating the Kingdom of Ends* (Cambridge, 1996), 153. "The Formulation of Humanity and its corollary, the vision of the Kingdom of Ends, provide an ideal to live up to as well as a long-term political and legal goal for humanity. But it is not feasible always to live up to this ideal, and where the attempt would make you a tool of evil, you should not do so" (144). Korsgaard believes that the truth-telling law associated with the Formulation of Humanity and the respect for humanity commanded by the vision of the Kingdom of Ends can conflict, and when they do one must forego the former.

There is something uncomfortable about her loophole. "Feasibility" is a moral measure to which Kant could not only never subscribe, but one which undermines his entire moral philosophy. In terms of this interpretation, pure imagination guided by the moral law would not serve as the measure, but empirical imagination guided by the anticipation of consequences would. This is the reason why there are no loopholes in the Kingdom of Ends.

I believe that the drawing model, while also allowing play in the application of the moral standard, preserves the unity of the Kantian approach far better. As I have said, no moral philosophy can give a clear answer to every single moral quandary. Would that life could be made so simple!

24. In my language here, we never encounter the field (as field) or any particular quantum (as quantum) upon it. These withdraw in order to allow the appearances that they structure to come forth at all. Although every appearance must conform to the conditions of the field, what actually occurs on the field is an entirely contingent matter.

25. Its corresponding idea, the world, serves merely (but necessarily and significantly) to regulate the understanding such that it seeks totality in the succession of (phenomenal) conditions.

26. Toward the beginning of his Appendix to *The Categorical Imperative*, H. J. Paton has anticipated such a closure based upon what he called "The Spontaneity of Mind." After recognizing the spontaneity of imagination in the sphere of knowledge, he moves to consideration of spontaneity with respect to the will. This he regards as a more challenging task, because "[i]n action the will works only with the form of law or universality, and it is therefore much more difficult to understand how its principle can be applied in the ordering of actions based upon given desires." See H. J. Paton, *The Categorical Imperative* (Chicago, 1948), 143.

Clearly, the schemata and the theoretical categories determine objects in ways unavailable to the will, which must always choose its maxims. But his otherwise astute analysis requires only an ascription of imagination in the practical realm in order to bring "the spontaneity of mind" to an appropriate unity.

2. THE CONCEPT OF AN OBJECT OF PURE PRACTICAL REASON

1. Deleuze quite rightly notes the revolutionary character of Kant's move here: "Kant reverses the relationship of the law and the Good, which is as important as the reversal of the movement-time relationship. It is the Good which depends on the law, and not vice versa." (In ancient times, Deleuze notes citing Plato, if men knew the Good they would not need

laws.) Gilles Deleuze, *Kant's Critical Philosophy,* trans. Hugh Tomlinson and Barbara Habberjam (Minneapolis, 1990).

He proceeds to liken the law's entirely formal nature and its consequent absence of content and directive to Kafka's *The Penal Colony* in that the law is "purely practical and not theoretical" (x, xi). Deleuze's own imaginative leap is surely provocative, and he is just as surely aware that this is quite excessive, not only because the theoretical apparatus for the law is quite extensively delineated, but also because in *The Penal Colony* Kafka is quite clearly setting aside any concern for humanity as an end in itself precisely in order to display it more shiningly.

2. See Immanuel Kant, *Religion within the Limits of Reason Alone,* trans. Theodore M. Greene and Hoyt H. Hudson (New York, 1960), 17–21 (for the German, see *Kants Werke. Akademie Textausgabe,* Band VI. [Berlin, 1968], 22–25).

3. See Hans Adolf Martin and Dieter Krallmann, eds., *Allgemeiner Kant-index zu Kants gesammelten Schriften,* Band 2 (Berlin, 1967), 900. There are very few uses in senses unconnected with "typic" in other places in Kant's works, but none at all in the other two critiques.

4. See Immanuel Kant, *Foundations of the Metaphysics of Morals,* trans. Lewis White Beck (Indianapolis and New York, 1978), where these function as three of Kant's four recurrent examples (the fourth is developing one's talents for the good of humanity).

5. In *Kant's Theory of Freedom* (Cambridge, 1993), Henry Allison argues that although both proclaimed agreement in principle, the differences were greater than acknowledged. According to Allison, for Kant the best moral state "is one in which reason controls and limits (but not really suppresses) the inclinations" while for Schiller "it is one in which the two exist in perfect harmony." In his discussion, Allison claims that Kant rejects resembling Schiller's "inclination toward duty" and ideal of a "beautiful soul." The latter in particular "represents a species of moral fanaticism" (181, 183).

However, it seems to me that Schiller is a far more rigorous Kantian than Allison (and others) give him credit for being. In *Über Anmut und Würde,* Schiller writes, "In the moral legislation of pure reason and in its natural legislation, a different necessity obtains in which neither one is permitted to effect accidental changes in the other. Thus even the most virtuous spirit, who takes a stand against sensibility, cannot suppress desire itself, but can merely refuse its determination of the will." Friedrich Schiller, *Sämtliche Werke,* Fünfter Band (München, 1960), 473–74, translation mine. This is virtually the same as Allison's characterization of Kant's view in the first citation in this note. Perhaps it might be better to conclude that the two great figures understood one another better than even so astute an interpreter as Allison, and that the two positions were in greater accord than they seemed.

6. That is, the synthesis of imagination produces the field of experience by giving the categories sense and significance, and it gives measure insofar as it determines the scope and limits of the field.

3. THE INCENTIVES (*TRIEBFEDER*) OF PURE PRACTICAL REASON

1. Some good reasons for leaving *Triebfeder* untranslated are given in an article by Larry Herrera. "Kant on the Moral *Triebfeder*," *Kant-Studien* 91, Heft 4 (2000). He cites Beck's discomfort with his own translation and his observation that any German would instantly grasp Kant's meaning (Lewis White Beck, *A Commentary to Kant's Critique of Practical Reason* [Chicago, 1960], 91). While it is not so clear to a reader of English, Herrera says that *Triebfeder* "denotes the driving or propelling force behind an action," 395n.

2. Although it may seem that the *Critique of Judgment* will add at least one more concept, the concept of purposiveness, to this very short list, it is not correct to say that this latter concept *determines* the feeling of pleasure and pain. Rather, it belongs to the reflective judgment, in accord with which pleasure and pain are experienced but not determined in certain ways (i.e., experienced as pleasant, as beautiful, as good).

3. Again, reason by itself generates nothing.

4. While there is much disagreement as to whether Kant had envisioned a critique of judgment at the time of his conception of the *Critique of Pure Reason,* or whether he intended to include both the will and pleasure/pain in his second critique, it does not affect the character of the first critique in its exclusion of these.

5. The two ways: (1) actions can be performed only in accordance with duty and not *from* duty (can be legal but not moral), and (2) actions can be *contra* duty.

6. A willfully false empirical judgment is an action *contra* duty, and so its ultimate practical component is clear.

7. For example, Beck begins his translation thusly: "Duty! Thou sublime and mighty name that dost embrace nothing charming or insinuating but requirest submission." Immanuel Kant, *Critique of Practical Reason*, trans. Lewis White Beck (Indianapolis and New York, 1956), 87. He follows Abbott closely (word for word at the outset), though a few minor changes are made in deference to the changes in usage that have occurred across the many decades. Abbott's translation first appeared in 1873. See *Kant's Critique of Prac-*

tical Reason and Other Works on the Theory of Ethics, trans. T. K. Abbott (London, 1963), 180. But strict adherence to the German (V, 86) yields the more prosaic yet more accurate: "*Duty!* You sublime great name that grasps nothing ingratiating (*Beliebtes*) and leads to nothing insinuating but rather demands submission."

8. This citation is from Immanuel Kant, *Critique of Judgment,* trans. J. H. Bernard (New York, 1951), 86.

9. "Hence, in transforming the ultimate metaphysical concerns of the human mind with the halo of sublimity and infinity, the critique does not merely put forth an abstract philosophical principle but, thereby, performs an act of profound cultural and existential implications." Yirmiahu Yovel, *Kant's Practical Philosophy Reconsidered* (Dordrecht and Boston, 1989), 144. Yovel has grasped the existential dimensions *already within* the Kantian moral philosophy as few others have. His "halo of sublimity and infinity" eloquently express the embeddedness of imagination in Kant's moral philosophy and the way pure images are at once vicarious images, images to be lived through.

10. The moral life includes within it the pursuit of truth belonging to the scientific life as well.

4. DIALECTIC OF PURE PRACTICAL REASON IN GENERAL AND IMAGINATION

1. Rosenstreich has astutely noted an irony issuing from the heterogeneity of the two ends: "Because of this competition in his system between happiness which connotes an outcome and the determination of the moral law which connotes an autarchic character of morality, Kant arrives at a paradoxical conclusion; he does not turn the—all too human—expectation of happiness into a vehicle for ethical action though . . . he takes many evil human deeds to be vehicles of that sort. Evil can serve the good, as war can serve peace, or competition can serve cooperation. But one alleged good, like happiness, is not made subservient to the real good which consists in the purity of the moral motive." Nathan Rosenstreich, *Practice and Realization: Studies in Kant's Moral Philosophy* (The Hague, 1979), 52–53.

In terms of this interpretation, the ultimate *moral* issue turns upon the priority of pure synthesis of imagination, which always yields the vicarious pure image of the highest good, over any and all empirical syntheses. Rosenstreich's analysis underscores the weakness of Korsgaard's above. The reading of "feasible" ignores the contingent quality of the outcomes of all human actions.

2. The relation between *Wille* and *Willkür* is not quite as straightfor-

ward as that, as Beck points out. See Lewis White Beck, *A Commentary to Kant's Critique of Practical Reason* (Chicago, 1960), 177n. Generally, as he points out, *Wille* is supposed to refer to the will as spontaneity, while *Willkür* refers to it as autonomy, although they are intertwined and often impossible to distinguish from one another in the Kantian text. A more recent discussion of this (still admittedly difficult) matter can be found in Henry Allison, *Kant's Theory of Freedom*, 129–36. His solution: "it is *Wille* in the narrow sense that provides the norm and *Willkür* that chooses in light of this norm" (130).

3. Here, no division into "mathematical" and "dynamical" antinomies is found. However, there is some parallel. The first ground-consequent relation, like the mathematical antinomies, is called "absolutely false." The second is only "conditionally false," and so could be true under certain conditions.

4. Rossvær has argued that "because between the faculties of reason and sensuousness there is a difference in kind . . . , Kant cannot justify the concept of the highest good as a synthesis of morality and happiness." Viggo Rossvær, *Kant's Moral Philosophy* (Oslo, 1979), 174. He opts rather for reading a social meaning into Kant's conception. However, it is precisely this heterogeneity that both allows for the synthesis of the two stems and requires the projection of their union into another life. Further, this heterogeneity has nothing to do with reason's ability to form maxims concerning happiness. Rossvær's interpretation is revealing in the sense that if imagination cannot enter the "divide" between sensibility and understanding, then it is difficult indeed to see how a highest good joining morality and happiness can be envisioned.

5. Guyer worries about the "non-natural" status of "the next life," and is at pains to show that the connection between morality and happiness is more intimate than it seems, and that (from a reading of certain passages in the Kantian text) happiness is at least possible *in this world* in proportion to worthiness. "At least as far as we can tell, all our needs to act arise solely from the fact that we are mortal, embodied creatures, although morality requires us to impose constraints of a reason that may itself be supranatural on these needs and desires . . . our happiness certainly and perhaps our moral perfection as well can only be achieved in nature, that is, within our existence as embodied creatures. The happiness included in the highest good must therefore be at least possible in human history, not somewhere else." Paul Guyer, *Kant on Freedom, Law and Happiness* (Cambridge, 2000), 390. But he need not worry so much. Kant's claim is not that he (and the rest of us) will have to await a problematic future life in order for there to be any hope of happiness. It is merely that we must be steadily mindful of our moral conduct, that

concern for happiness can undermine this mindfulness, and that whether we actually achieve happiness or not in nature is largely out of our hands. If fortune breaks his way, Guyer may be turn out to be happiest of us all— whether or not he has reason constrain his embodied needs and desires.

5. IMAGINATION AND THE POSTULATES OF IMMORTALITY AND GOD

1. Ricoeur regards the matter of such hope as central to the Kantian ethical project. It has both a structural role in the thought of the completion of the will, and it extends the substantive content of Kant's strictly moral philosophy into the philosophy of religion. A further kinship obtains between Kant's question "What may I hope for?" and its treatment in the Platonic dialogues. Socrates also exhorts those who voted for his acquittal to "be of good hope (εὐέλπιδας) when facing death" (41c). Kantian immortality is therefore an aspect of our need to effectuate the highest good in reality; now this temporality, this 'progress toward the infinite,' is not in our power; we can only 'encounter' it (*antreffen*). It is in this sense that the postulate of freedom expresses the face of hope of the postulate of freedom." Paul Ricoeur, "Freedom in the Light of Hope," trans. Robert Sweeney, in *The Conflict of Interpretations: Essays in Hermeneutics*, ed. Don Ihde (Evanston, Ill., 1974), 420. This creative and thoughtful reader of Kant also does not employ the term "imagination" in his hermeneutics. I wonder whether a good case for its silently animating presence can also be made here.

2. However, I do not think they are fundamentally different at all. The primary issue in both is not immortality but *goodness*, which requires living out *this* life in the best possible way.

3. Chalier describes an equally strange Levinasian religion in her comparative study of Kant and Levinas: Levinas sees "the sign of an extraordinary God, who, without promising anything . . . arrives and becomes, thanks to the response to those he elects for unremitting service. Such is the call to holiness and responsibility. It does not depend on an *idea* of humanity but on the attention paid to every singularity, since it is upon that singularity—and through it alone—that the idea of humanity takes on a universal sense." Catherine Chalier, *What Ought I to Do: Morality in Kant and Levinas*, trans. Jane Marie Todd (Ithaca, N.Y., and London, 2002), 175.

4. Such a religion can be here designated by the name "aesthetic religion" in name only. Its "congregants" have been indicated in name earlier as "images of freedom" and as "unique works of art."

5. Indeed, he criticizes Greek ethical thought of all stripes for its appar-

ent conviction that virtue can be achieved without the postulate of God as object of belief for this purpose (V, 126f).

6. IMAGINATION AND THE MORAL EXTENSION OF REASON

1. Here, Kant's view is (no doubt unconsciously) close to the one found in Plato's *Meno*, where Socrates initially deflects the question of whether virtue is inborn and acquired and ultimately concludes that it can be neither. Perhaps Socrates' mythical answer that virtue comes by "divine dispensation" is more akin than it might seem to Kant's view concerning the darkness of freedom's ultimate origin.

2. The extended treatment of the concept of God regards matters that tend not to be of central interest to many of us who philosophize today. However, Kant's restriction of the concept of God to the moral realm, and its consequent exclusion from the realm of physics on one side and from that of theology on the other, is entirely in line with the notion of a vicarious image in service to a life lived within the appropriately human limits that I am here suggesting.

3. He does not argue in precisely this manner, choosing instead to focus on the fallaciousness of the inference to, e.g., a deity as the source of order and design in nature. However, the basis for his argument is the restriction of pure reason to objects of the senses.

7. METHODOLOGY OF PURE PRACTICAL REASON

1. For a commentary on this division of the *Critique of Pure Reason*, see my master's thesis, Freydberg. "Kant's Transcendental Doctrine of Method" (University of Michigan, 1976).

2. Most famous is the *noble lie*, in which the citizens were told that they were fashioned under the earth and divided there into three classes (414d–415e), but also quite remarkable are the many lies required (459c–d) to regulate the sexual mixing of the guardians.

3. Kant also declares that this happiness must accord with worthiness in the first critique.

4. Kant warns especially against esteeming "so-called *noble* [supermeritorious] actions" (V, 158, emphasis in original), since these may encourage actions done from a motive other than duty, even when they do no other harm.

5. In this light one can understand the superior status generally accorded to tragedy, especially Greek tragedy, although in my view comedy (espe-

cially Old Comedy) discloses our nature equally well by presenting moral norms in its very deed of flouting them. The noble suffering of an Antigone cannot be directly compared to the initial small-mindedness of a Strepsiades, although both *Antigone* and *Clouds* have the same point, namely the need of human beings to honor their moral obligations.

6. The first step is to make a habit of judging according to moral laws, including the distinction between "essential" and "non-essential" duties and the distinction between morally correct actions (those done in accord with the law) and actions having moral worth (those done from the law itself).

The second step "lies in calling to notice the purity of will by a vivid exhibition of the moral disposition in examples" (V, 160). This final step provides "a consciousness of an independence from all inclinations and circumstances and of the possibility of being sufficient (*genug*) onto myself, which is salutary for me in other respects" (V, 161).

7. This notion of beauty, of course, foreshadows much of the subject matter of the *Critique of Judgment*. Contrary to those who maintain that there is a radical break between the first two critiques and the third, this passage testifies to the contrary, namely that the concerns of the *Critique of Judgment* are already embedded here.

CONCLUSION(S)

1. A short textual analysis and defense of this view can be found in my "Concerning 'Syntheses of Understanding' in the B Deduction," in *Proceedings of the Eighth International Kant Congress*, vol. II, pt. I, ed. Hoke Robinson (Milwaukee, 1995), 287–94. "Concerning 'Syntheses of Imagination' in the B Deduction."

2. While Kant never developed what we would today consider a full philosophy of language, I maintain that an imagination-guided interpretation of the critical philosophy at key points would yield an account of language that presents a formidable challenge to contemporary continental directions as well as to Anglo-American approaches. In this note, I can only gesture toward such an account and toward such challenges.

A crucial sentence in §19 of the Transcendental Deduction in the *Critique of Pure Reason* reads, "I find that judgment is nothing but the manner in which given cognitions (*Erkenntnisse*) are brought to the *objective* unity of apperception. This is what the little relation-word (*Verhältniswörtchen*) aims toward" (B141–42, emphasis in original).

In judgment considered in its totality, the "*is*" gathers the categories, the pure productive synthesis of imagination, pure intuition—in a word, the principles (*Grundsätze*)—the conditions for the possibility of experience—

and whatever occurs in accord with them on the field, or in more Kantian terms, in experience. When we abstract from these conditions, the result—very broadly speaking—is either one based upon formal logic, or it is a mix of strategies, digressions, margins, differends, and the like. Even when the copula does not appear expressly, it is present in the depths. We can philosophize in terms of the latter alternatives only, I say, by tacitly presupposing the Kantian subsoil as interpreted along the lines I here suggest. For example, Lyotard writes, "A differend, I say, and not a litigation. It is not that humans are mean or that their interests or passions are antagonistic. On the same score of what is not human . . . they are situated in heterogeneous phrase regimens and are taken hold of by stakes tied to heterogeneous genres of discourse." Jean-François Lyotard, *The Differend: Phrases in Dispute*, trans. Georges Van Den Abbeele (Minneapolis, 1988), 140.

My disagreement with this approach is fundamental, but I do not deny in the least that the work of Lyotard, or that certain texts of Derrida, for example, break the mold of traditional narration and provide not only provocative but also valuable avenues of interpretation. I do, however, deny that the imaginative apparatus to which Kant points is merely one "genre of discourse" among others, or is a "metanarrative" that can no longer be accepted or sustained. "We are taken hold of by stakes tied to" imagination and the ruling image of unity, whatever else holds us. Otherwise, we could not distinguish phrases, genres, geneses, or anything else.

Interestingly, my difference with the celebrated Anglo-American philosopher Quine is similar. He writes, "If in some language we are at a loss to arrive at a satisfactory contextual translation of 'there is,' and hence of existential quantification, then we are at a loss to assess the ontology of the speakers of that language. . . . To entertain the notion of an ontology at all, known or unknown, for the speakers of such a language would be an unwarranted projection on our part of a parochial category appropriate to our linguistic circle." W. V. Quine, *Pursuit of Truth* (Cambridge, 1990), 28. We could not distinguish "our linguistic circle" from that of others, we could not discern contexts, we could not formulate a quantificational logic or a logic of any kind without the at least nascent workings of productive imagination.

EPILOGUE

1. Kant to K. L. Reinhold, Dec. 28–31, 1787. See Arnulf Zweig, ed. and trans., *Kant's Philosophical Correspondence* (Chicago, 1967), 127–28.

2. It is now available as *First Introduction to the Critique of Judgment*, trans. James Haden (Indianapolis and New York, 1965).

3. For example, Makkreel advocates a non-synthetic, orientational view

of imagination with its idea of wholeness as a hermeneutical signpost. See Rudolf Makkreel, *Imagination and Interpretation in Kant* (Chicago, 1990). This idea relies entirely upon the *synthetic* notions of purposive unity and systematic wholeness for its very conception.

With more flourish but even less connection with Kantian philosophy, Deleuze and Guattari write, "Kant's *Critique of Judgment* is an unrestrained work of old age, which his successors have still not caught up with: all the mind's faculties overcome their limits, the very limits that Kant had so carefully laid down in his prime" (Gilles Deleuze and Felix Guattari, *What Is Philosophy?* trans. Hugh Tomlinson and Graham Burchell [New York, 1994], 2). It is difficult to be completely mistaken in philosophy, but Deleuze and Guatteri—two thinkers who have my respect—have succeeded in doing so with this comment. When the role of imagination, which is determinative in the first two critiques where the synthesis of concepts takes place, and in the third where the relation of the free imagination and understanding takes place, the unity of the three critiques comes sharply into view. In the *Critique of Judgment* (the critique of the faculty of pleasure and pain), Kant is just as "careful" not to ascribe a single capability to the "mind" than is found in the first two critiques.

4. Single *function* refers to the function of bringing to the unity under a concept. Deeply concealed syntheses underlie this single function. Single does not mean simple.

5. Taking as our example Mozart's *Zauberflöte*, we might say, "This opera is a divine gift" to denote a concept to which an intuition could never correspond, or more prosaically, "this opera is a balm" to denote a concept that points to a possible intuition.

6. The other parts of the analogy concern, in general, (1) immediacy, (2) disinterest, and (4) universality. In every case, the non-conceptual judgment of beauty is reflective; its conceptual counterpart is determinative (V, 353–54).

BIBLIOGRAPHY

Abbott, T. K. *Kant's Critique of Practical Reason and Other Works on the Theory of Ethics.* London: Longmans, 1963.

Allison, Henry. *Kant's Theory of Freedom.* Cambridge: Cambridge University Press, 1993.

Arendt, Hannah. *Lectures on Kant's Political Philosophy.* Ed. Ronald Beiner. Chicago: University of Chicago Press, 1982.

———. *The Life of the Mind.* Vol. 2: *Willing.* New York and London: Harcourt Brace Jovanovich, 1978.

Beck, Lewis White. *A Commentary to Kant's Critique of Practical Reason.* Chicago: University of Chicago Press, 1960.

———. *Early German Philosophy.* Cambridge: Cambridge University Press, 1969.

Chalier, Catherine. *What I Ought to Do: Morality in Kant and Levinas.* Trans. Jane Marie Todd. Ithaca, N.Y., and London: Cornell University Press, 2002.

Deleuze, Gilles. *Kant's Critical Philosophy.* Trans. Hugh Tomlinson and Barbara Habberjam. Minneapolis: University of Minnesota Press, 1990.

Deleuze, Gilles, and Felix Guattari. *What Is Philosophy?* Trans. Hugh Tomlinson and Graham Burchell. New York: Columbia University Press, 1994.

Derrida, Jacques. "Passions: 'An Oblique Offering.'" Trans. David Wood. In *Derrida: A Critical Reader,* ed. David Wood, Oxford: Blackwell, 1992.

———. "Tympan." In *Margins of Philosophy,* trans. Alan Bass. Chicago: University of Chicago Press, 1982.

Findler, Richard. "Kant's Phenomenological Ethics." *Research in Phenomenology* XXVII (1998).

Freydberg, Bernard. "Anglo-American Kant." *History of European Ideas* 21, no. 1 (1995).

———. "Concerning 'Syntheses of Understanding' in the B Deduction." In *Proceedings of the Eighth International Kant Congress,* vol. II, pt. I. Edited by Hoke Robinson. 287–94. Milwaukee: Marquette University Press, 1995.

———. *Imagination and Depth in Kant's Critique of Pure Reason.* New York: Peter Lang, 1994.

———. "Kant's Transcendental Doctrine of Method." Master's thesis, University of Michigan, 1976.

——. *Provocative Form in Plato, Kant, Nietzsche (and Others)*. New York: Peter Lang, 2000.

——. "Revisiting the 'Transcendental Deduction' in the Dialectic of the *Critique of Pure Reason.*" In *Akten des IX. Internationalen Kant-Kongresses*, Band 2: *Kant und die Berliner Erklärung*. Berlin: de Gruyter, 2001.

Gregor, Mary. *Laws of Freedom*. Oxford: Blackwell, 1963.

Guyer, Paul, ed. *The Cambridge Companion to Kant*. Cambridge: Cambridge University Press, 1992.

——. *Kant on Freedom, Law and Happiness*. Cambridge: Cambridge University Press, 2000.

Heidegger, Martin. *Kant und das Problem der Metaphysik*. Frankfurt am Main: V. Klostermann, 1965.

Herman, Barbara. *The Practice of Moral Judgment*. Cambridge: Cambridge University Press, 1993.

Herrera, Larry. "Kant on the Moral *Triebfeder.*" *Kant-Studien* 91, Heft 4 (2000).

Hume, David. *An Enquiry concerning Human Understanding*, in L. A. Selby-Bigge, ed., *Hume's Enquiries, Second Edition*. Oxford: Oxford at the Clarendon Press, 1902.

Kant, Immanuel. *Anthropology from a Pragmatic Point of View*. Trans. Mary Gregor. The Hague: Kluwer Academic Publishers, 1974.

——. *Critique of Judgment*. Trans. J. H. Bernard. New York: Hafner, 1951.

——. *Critique of Practical Reason*. Trans. Lewis White Beck. Indianapolis and New York: Library of Liberal Arts, 1956.

——. *Critique of Pure Reason*. Trans. Norman Kemp Smith. New York: St. Martin's Press, 1929.

——. *First Introduction to the Critique of Judgment*. Trans. James Haden. Indianapolis and New York: Library of Liberal Arts, 1965.

——. *Foundations of the Metaphysics of Morals*. Trans. Lewis White Beck. Indianapolis and New York: Library of Liberal Arts, 1959.

——. *Kant's Gesammelte Schriften*. Band 27. Berlin: W. de Gruyter, 1974.

——. *Kant's Philosophical Correspondence*. Ed. and trans. Arnulf Zweig. Chicago: University of Chicago Press, 1967.

——. *Kants Werke, Akademie Textausgabe*. Band V. Berlin: de Gruyter, 1968.

——. *Lectures on Ethics*. Trans. Peter Heath. Cambridge: Cambridge University Press, 1997.

——. *Religion within the Limits of Reason Alone*. Trans. Theodore M. Greene and Hoyt H. Hudson. New York: Harper Torchbooks, 1960.

Kemp Smith, Norman. *A Commentary to Kant's Critique of Pure Reason*. New York: Humanities Press, 1962.

Kerstein, Samuel J. *Kant's Search for the Supreme Principle of Morality.* Cambridge: Cambridge University Press, 2000.

Korsgaard, Christine. *Creating the Kingdom of Ends.* Cambridge: Cambridge University Press, 1996.

Levinas, Emmanuel. *Otherwise than Being.* Pittsburgh: Duquesne University Press, 1998.

———. *Totality and Infinity.* Trans. Alfonso Lingis. Pittsburgh: Duquesne University Press, 1969.

Lingis, Alphonso. *The Imperative.* Bloomington: Indiana University Press, 1998.

Llewelyn, John. *HypoCritical Imagination: Between Kant and Levinas.* London and New York: Routledge, 2000.

Longuenesse, Beatrice. *Kant and the Capacity to Judge: Sensibility and Discursivity in the Transcendental Analytic.* Trans. Charles T. Wolfe. Princeton and Oxford: Princeton University Press, 2002.

Lyotard, Jean François. *The Differend: Phrases in Dispute.* Trans. Georges Van Den Abbeele. Minneapolis: University of Minnesota Press, 1988.

Makkreel, Rudolf. *Imagination and Interpretation in Kant.* Chicago: University of Chicago Press, 1990.

Martin, Hans Adolf, and Dieter Krallman. *Allgemeiner Kantindex ʒu Kants gesammelten Schriften.* Band 2. Berlin: de Gruyter, 1967.

O'Neill, Onora. *Constructions of Reason: Explorations of Kant's Moral Philosophy.* Cambridge: Cambridge University Press, 1989.

Paton, H. J. *The Categorical Imperative.* Chicago: University of Chicago Press, 1948.

Plato. *Platonis Opera.* Vols. I–III. Ed. John Burnet. Oxford: Oxford University Press, 1995.

Quine, W. V. *Pursuit of Truth.* Cambridge: Cambridge University Press, 1990.

Ricoeur, Paul. *Freedom and Nature: The Voluntary and the Involuntary.* Trans. Erazim V. Kohák. Evanston, Ill.: Northwestern University Press, 1966.

———. "Freedom in the Light of Hope." Trans. Robert Sweeney. In *The Conflict of Interpretations: Essays in Hermeneutics,* ed. Don Ihde. Evanston, Ill.: Northwestern University Press, 1974.

Robinson, Hoke, ed. *Proceedings of the Eighth International Kant Congress.* Vol. II. Milwaukee: Marquette University Press, 1995.

Rosenstreich, Nathan. *Practice and Realization: Studies in Kant's Moral Philosophy.* The Hague: M. Nijhoff, 1979.

Rossvær, Viggo. *Kant's Moral Philosophy.* Oslo: Universitetsforl., 1979.

Sallis, John. *The Gathering of Reason.* Athens: Ohio University Press, 1980.

———. *Spacings—of Reason and Imagination in Texts of Kant, Fichte, Hegel.* Chicago: University of Chicago Press, 1987.

Schalow, Frank. *Imagination: Heidegger's Retrieval of the Kantian Ethic*. Lanham, Md.: University Press of America, 1986.

Schiller, Friedrich. *Sämtliche Werke*. Fünfter Band. München: Hanser, 1960.

Williams, T. C. *The Concept of the Categorical Imperative*. Oxford: Clarendon Press, 1968.

Wood, Allen. *Kant's Ethical Thought*. Cambridge: Cambridge University Press, 1999.

Yovel, Yirmiahu. *Kant's Practical Philosophy Reconsidered*. Dordrecht and Boston: Kluwer Academic, 1989.

Zweig, Arnulf, ed. and trans. *Kant's Philosophical Correspondence*. Chicago, 1967.

INDEX OF SUBJECTS

INDEX OF PERSONS

Index of Persons

BERNARD FREYDBERG is Professor of Philosophy at Slippery Rock University. He is author of Imagination and Depth in Kant's *Critique of Pure Reason; The Play of the Platonic Dialogues;* and *Provocative Form in Plato, Kant, Nietzsche (and Others).*